THE A.B.C.
OF
HIGHLAND DANCING
&
GAMES DIRECTORY

This is a glossary of words, names
and terms continually being used throughout the
Highland Dancing world. It has been compiled,
in alphabetical order, by the Technical Committee of
The Scottish Official Highland Dancing Association,
to assist the young dancer who may be about to
sit a theoretical examination or test — and in some
cases, to refresh the memory of the advanced
dancer or dancing teacher who may have let
the correct expression fall by the wayside.

The two sections that follow give information
about Highland Games that are staged in
Scotland and throughout the world.

Published **KINMOR MUSIC**
1994

For further information, please contact:
The Secretary of S.O.H.D.A.
Helen Virtue
8 Limegrove, North Berwick, East Lothian, EH39 5NN, Scotland

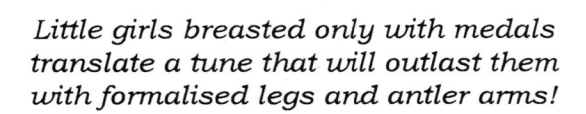

Little girls breasted only with medals translate a tune that will outlast them with formalised legs and antler arms!

Norman MacCaig (b. 1910), on Highland Games

© **Kinmor Music** 1994

Published by
Kinmor Music
Shillinghill, Temple, Midlothian, Scotland.

ISBN 0 9511204 6 8
File under: Dance/Sports General/Music and Folklore

Contents

Foreword

Glossary
1 - 57

Highland Games Directory
Scotland
61 - 84

Overseas
87 - 111

FOREWORD

The A.B.C. of Highland Dancing and Games Directory, being the first publication of its kind, is the culmination of many months of research done by the Technical Committee of the Scottish Official Highland Dancing Association (S.O.H.D.A.).

This book offers to its readers, in a single publication, an unsurpassed wealth of information which will be of interest not only to the dance enthusiast in particular, but will also prove to be a valuable asset to those interested in the Highland Games Circuit Worldwide.

Although primarily aimed at the Highland Dance enthusiast, it will also be of considerable interest to those engaged in other dance disciplines, describing as it does various movements in common with different types of dance. This publication will also prove to be an invaluable "tool" to those candidates preparing for Dance Examinations.

As the term A.B.C. indicates, this publication is set out in an easy-to-follow, logical sequence, describing as it does: Dance Movements, Dance History, Body Anatomy connected with Dance, Dance Associations, Definitions in Music, Highland Dress, Highland Games, Dance Positions, Dance Titles, etc., etc.

As is usually the case when a venture of this kind is embarked upon by a group of individuals, certain members of the group often emerge and play a distinctive role in the research and gathering together of relevant information. The compilation of this publication has been no exception. Consequently I would like to give special mention to two individuals without whose input and untiring efforts this publication would not have been possible; they are Charlie Mill from Dundee, a member of the S.O.H.D.A. Technical Division and a well-known personality on the Highland Games Circuit, and Mats Melin of the Stockholm Caledonian Dance Circle, a keen and very knowledgeable enthusiast of both Highland, Step-Dancing and Scottish Country Dancing whose organisation is affiliated with the S.O.H.D.A.

Finally, as I said at the beginning, this is the first publication of its kind. It is only the beginning, as the S.O.H.D.A. Technical Committee will keep its contents under review with the aim of constantly bringing it up to date and issuing new and complimentary publications.

Yours in Dance

Alex McGuire

President S.O.H.D.A.

the a.b.c of highland dancing and games directory

A

Aberchirder — Highland Games, usually held the second Saturday in August.

Aberdeen — Highland Games, usually held the third Sunday in June.

Aberfeldy — Highland Games, usually held the second Saturday in August.

Aberlour — Highland Games, usually held the first Saturday in August.

Abernethy — Highland Games, usually held the third Saturday in August (see Nethybridge).

Aboyne — Highland Games, usually held the first Saturday in August.

Aboyne Dress — Worn by girl dancers while performing the Hebridean and National Dances. Consisting of a blouse, velvet scalloped tunic, and tartan circular skirt over underskirts, it was inaugurated at the Aboyne Games in the 1950s to accompany the dance "Flora MacDonald's Fancy," which was introduced as a competitive dance, and the outfit has since been named the Aboyne Dress.

Addressing the Sword (First step of "Sword Dance") — The name given to the opening step. Legend claims that Highland chiefs of old placed the sword and scabbard to mark the field of battle, the opening step circling the possible plans and manoeuvres, while the remaining steps contained the execution and battle itself.

Adirondack — Highland Games, usually held the first Saturday in June in New York, U.S.A.

Adjudicator — An individual who is qualified through practical experience and theoretical examination, to judge Highland Dancers in competition.

Accent — An expression placed on any individual beat in a musical bar.

Achilles Tendon — This is the thick tendon connecting the foot and heel to the calf muscle. If damaged, it will most likely become inflamed. The best remedy is to rest it completely then gradually exercise to strengthen it.

Aerial Position — occurs when the working foot is raised off the ground to a given height.

Affiliated — A uniting of 2 or more associations or societies for the mutual benefit of further companionship and education. See V.S.U., S.C.D.C. and H.&N.D.A.

Airdrie — Highland Games, usually held the first Sunday in June.

Airth — Highland Games, usually held the fourth Saturday in July.

the a.b.c of highland dancing and games directory

Akimbo (First arm position in "Sailors' Hornpipe") — As in the usual Highland Dance position, or with straight fingers aimed down and to the front, the index finger resting on the hips with both thumbs to the rear at waist level. As the sailor of yesteryear worked continuously with tar, the outside edge of each hand is raised to prevent the sailor's "tarred" palms from coming in touch with the tunic. The elbows face directly to the side.

Alabama — Highland Games, usually held the fourth Saturday in September in Alabama, U.S.A.

Alaska — Highland Games, usually held in early August in Alaska, U.S.A.

Alexandria— Scottish Fair, usually held the third Saturday in September in Virginia, U.S.A.

Alma — Highland Games, usually held the fourth weekend in May in Michigan, U.S.A.

Alternative Step — A choice of step for the Highland Dancer to select. The Alternative Step covers the same number of musical bars as the original step and should be more or less a replica of the basic formation with a slight variation in certain movements and positions.

Alva — Highland Games, usually held the second Saturday in July.

Amherst — Scottish Festival, usually held the third Saturday in September in New York, U.S.A.

Ankle — The joint which connects the foot with the leg.

Annapolis Valley — Highland Games, usually held the fourth Saturday in August in Nova Scotia, Canada.

Anne Arundel — Scottish Festival, usually held the second Saturday in October in Maryland, U.S.A.

Antigonish — Highland Games, usually held the first Saturday in July in Nova Scotia, Canada.

Appeal — To demand another judgment on a higher level over a dispute on a dancing decision.

Apron — Or front of kilt, on which rests the sporran, kilt pin, etc.

Apron ("Irish Jig") — As part of the ladies "Irish Jig" costume, a small white cotton apron is worn round the waist and tied at the back. It may be trimmed with white lace, but kept as unornate as possible — no sequins or bows!

Arbroath — Highland Games, usually held the second Sunday in July.

Ardrossan — Highland Games, usually held the second Sunday in June.

Argyll Broadswords — A dance in Strathspey and Reel tempo, originating in the county of Argyll, for four dancers, traditionally male, and performed over four swords, placed at right angles, point to point. See S.O.H.D.A. Dance Sheet No. 2.

Argyllshire Gathering — Highland Games, usually held the fourth Thursday in August at Oban.

Arisaig — Highland Games, usually held the fourth Wednesday in July.

Arizona — Highland Games, usually held the third Saturday in February in Arizona, U.S.A.

Arm Positions — There are five basic arm positions the dancer uses when performing. In all Highland Dances the opposite arm to the working foot is raised — when both feet are used simultaneously (IE, High-Cutting, Backstepping, Rocking, etc.), both arms are raised (See Finger Grouping). The five basic arm positions are as follows -

1st Position — The hands are placed lightly on the hips, knuckles against the body, back of hands facing front. Both wrists are held firm with elbows positioned directly to the sides.

2nd Position — The working arm is lifted at the side, with a gentle bending of both wrist and arm. The working arm is positioned over and slightly forward of the head, with the palm facing inwards. The other arm is placed in 1st position.

3rd Position — Both arms are raised as for 2nd position, the palms facing inwards towards each other.

4th Position — As for 3rd Position, with both hands positioned closer and slightly higher and the fingers almost touching.

5th Position — The hands are slightly curved down in front of the body, the hands quite close together and the little fingers almost touching the kilt.

Assemble — A motion of specified height started on the ball of one foot and ended at the same time on the balls of both feet in a specified position, IE., 3rd or 5th Position.

Associate Teacher — A position attained through practical and theoretical examination by dancers aged 16 to 18, allowing them to start a dancing class and after a short training period to adjudicate at indoor competitions.

Assynt — See Lochinver.

Athena — Caledonian Games, usually held the second Saturday in July in Oregon, U.S.A.

Atlanta — Celtic Festival, usually held at the end of April in Atlanta, Georgia, U.S.A.

Auckland — Highland Games, usually held the fourth Saturday in November in Auckland, North Island, New Zealand.

Aurora — Highland Games, usually held the third Saturday in May in Colorado, U.S.A.

Aviemore — Highland Games, usually held the fourth Sunday in July.

B

Baby — Term used to describe the group in which a young dancer (up to the age of seven years) competes.

Backstep — (One Backstep occupies one beat of music) — With the RF in 3rd Aerial Position, pass the RF, as in shedding, to 3rd Rear Aerial Position. Slide the RF down the back of the L leg, spring on to the RF and slide the LF up the front of the R leg to 3rd Aerial Position. Repeat as required.

Bagpipes — A wind instrument consisting of a bag fitted with pipes — played by a piper to accompany Highland Dancers.

Balance — (Occupying 2 beats of music) — With the RF extended out to 4th Intermediate Aerial Position, bring the RF in to 5th Position to displace the LF out to 4th Rear Intermediate Aerial Position (Count 1). Bring the LF in to 5th Rear Position to displace the RF out to 4th Intermediate Aerial Position (Count 2). Repeat as required.

Ball — When the foot is placed on the ball, the ball of the foot along with the pads of the toes touch the ground.

Ball Position — is one in which the heel, or heels, is/are raised off the floor and the weight is taken on the ball of the foot or feet. The "ball" of the supporting foot is used throughout while dancing.

Ballater — Highland Games, usually held the second Thursday in August.

Ball-Change — A quick weight change from the ball of one foot to the ball of the other in a specified position, IE., 3rd or 5th Position.

Ball-Dig (Movement in "Sailors' Hornpipe") — An acute beat executed with the ball of the working foot in a specified position.

Balloch — Highland Games, usually held the third Saturday in July.

Balloné (Occupying 2 beats of music) — With the RF extended out to 4th Intermediate Aerial Position, hop on the LF and, using a circular knee action, bring the RF halfway between 4th Intermediate Aerial Position and 3rd Aerial Position (Count 1). Beat the ball of the RF in 3rd or 5th Position (Count and). Beat the ball of the LF in 5th Rear Position, extending the RF out to 4th Intermediate Aerial Position (Count 2). Similar to "Syncopated Hop."

Balmoral — A flat Scottish bonnet worn by male dancers as part of the Highland Dress.

Banchory — Highland Games, usually held the fourth Saturday in July.

Bar — In the writing of music the sections of staff are divided by vertical lines called bar lines into divisions of equal duration — each division adopting the same duration of time.

Barra, Isle of — Highland Games, usually held the second Tuesday in July.

Barracks, Johnnie (Wilt Thou Go To The ...) — A solo Highland Dance of 8 steps in 2/4 tempo (originally 6/8 tempo danced to the tune of "Cock O´The North"). See S.O.H.D.A. Dance Sheet No. 11.

Barre — A horizontal rail fixed to the wall at waist level, which dancers use to balance themselves while exercising.

Basic Movement — occurs when two or more basic positions are joined together.

Basic Positions — All dance movements are based on the positions of the feet, head, arms and overall deportment..

Basic Step — occurs when basic movements are joined together.

Basque (Pas de) — A common step of the Basque people in the Pyrenees — regularly used in folk dances throughout many countries of the world.

Bathgate — Highland Games, usually held the fourth Saturday in May.

Bearsden & Milngavie — Highland Games, usually held the second Saturday in June.

Beat — A steady, uniform vibration or one of equal value in a musical bar.

Beating — The raising of either foot off the ground and replacing the weight carried beforehand on the foot to the ground without body motion.

Beginner — Term used to categorise the first section in which a dancer competes from the age of seven.

Bellbottoms — Trousers, worn usually by sailors, that widen towards the ankle. This enabled them to be easily rolled up when the sailor was swabbing decks, etc.

Bellingham — Highland Games, usually held the first Saturday in June in Washington, U.S.A.

Belt — A broad band of leather (usually black) fastened by an ornamental buckle worn by the male Highland Dancer as part of the Highland outfit.

Big Bear Lake — Scottish Festival and Games, usually held the last Saturday in June in California, U.S.A.

Billings — Highland Games, usually held the second Saturday in June in Montana, U.S.A.

Birnam — Highland Games, usually held the fourth Saturday in August.

Blackford — Highland Games, usually held the fourth Saturday in May.

Blair Atholl — Highland Games, usually held the fourth Sunday in May.

Blairgowrie — Highland Games, usually held the first Sunday in September.

Blairmore — Highland Games, usually held the second Saturday in June.

Blantyre — Highland Games, usually held the second Sunday in June.

Blue Bonnets Over The Border — A solo Hebridean step dance of 6 steps in 6/8 tempo, collected in South Uist in the Outer Hebrides. See S.O.H.D.A. Dance Sheet No. 28.

Blue Ridge — Scottish Festival, usually held the second weekend in September in Virginia, U.S.A.

Boards — A flat wooden structure, raised slightly above the ground level, measuring not less than 24 feet by 18 feet, on which dancers perform and compete.

Boat Rocking (Arm movement in "Sailors' Hornpipe") — An action where the arms, in 2nd Folded Position, dip in motion with the roll of the body, indicating the ship rolling in and over the waves.

Bobby Cuthbertson — A solo dance of 6 steps in 2/4 Reel time. The dance was devised in the late 1950s by Charlie Mill of Dundee in honour of his former dancing teacher Robert McNiven Cuthbertson, who was instrumental in forming the Scottish Official Highland Dancing Association in 1947. See S.O.H.D.A. Dance Sheet No. 15.

Body Roll (Action in "Sailors' Hornpipe") — A motion where the roll of the body develops naturally from the feet and arm movements, representing the roll of the wind-blown ship. E.G., used during the 2nd step, when the dancer's body may "roll" with the motion of the working foot.

Bo'ness — Highland Games, usually held the first Saturday in June.

Bonnie Brae — Highland Games, usually held the second Saturday in June in New Jersey, U.S.A.

Bonnie Breist Knot — A solo Scottish step dance of 7 steps in 2/4 tempo. The formation and design of the steps describe the basic shape of a "Lover's Knot," IE, Bows, Ties, Knot, etc. See S.O.H.D.A. Dance Sheet No. 19.

Bonnie Dundee — A solo Scottish step dance of 11 steps in 6/8 tempo. This dance is based on the original dance devised in the mid-nineteenth century by the late David Anderson, a well-known dancing master from Dundee, who originally arranged the steps to the tune "Highland Laddie." See S.O.H.D.A. Dance Sheet No. 23.

Bonnyrigg Rose — Highland Games, usually held the second week in June.

Bourrée (Movement used in National Dances) — A movement comprising three small steps on the balls of the feet, travelled to the side away from the commencing foot. The motion can be started with an extension, or with a small hop on the supporting foot.

> **Bourrée Devant** — Three small steps on the balls of the feet travelling to the side away from the starting foot as follows: 5th Position; towards 2nd Position; then again 5th Position (Front-Side-Front).

> **Bourrée Derrière** — Three small steps on the balls of the feet travelling to the side away from the starting foot as follows: 5th Rear Position; towards 2nd Position; then again 5th Rear Position (Behind-Side-Behind).

> **Bourrée Under** — Three small steps on the balls of the feet travelling to the side away from the starting foot as follows: 5th Rear Position; towards 2nd Position; 5th Position (Behind-Side-Front).

> **Bourrée Over** — Three small steps on the balls of the feet travelling to the side away from the starting foot as follows: 5th Position; towards 2nd Position; then 5th Rear Position (Front-Side-Behind).

Bow — A movement to signify the start and finish of a dance. With the head, arms and feet in 1st Position, incline the body forward slowly and return to original position.

Bow-Tie — A knotted neck-tie worn with the Prince Charlie Coatee by the male Highland Dancer as part of the Highland outfit.

Braemar — Highland Games, usually held the first Saturday in September.

Braid — A flat length of narrow fabric of three or more closely-intertwined threads made in various fancy patterns and used for trimming, binding or outlining — used on the edgings of a Highland Dancer's doublet.

Break — A recurring sequence of movements usually executed at the finish of every half-step.

Breeches — A garment worn during the "Irish Jig" by male dancers on the lower parts of the body, as distinguished from trousers, coming just below the knee.

Bridge of Allan (Strathallan) — Highland Games, usually held the first Sunday in August.

B.A.T.D. (The British Associations of Teachers of Dancing) — Although not a "specialist" Highland Dancing Association, the B.A.T.D. do have, amongst other branches of dance, a Highland Branch which organises examination and teacher certificate tests in Highland and National Dances.

Brodick — Highland Games, usually held the first Saturday in August.

Brogues — A stout pair of leather outdoor shoes, whose long laces are usually criss-crossed round the ankles and tied on the outer side of each calf muscle. They are worn by males as part of the outdoor Highland dress outfit.

Brush — See Inward and Outward Brush.

Burghead — Highland Games, usually held the fourth Sunday in June.

Burntisland — Highland Games, usually held the third Monday in July.

Bute — Highland Games, usually held the third Saturday in August.

C

Cable Haul (Arm movement in "Sailors' Hornpipe") — An action where both arms are reached forward diagonally and "imaginary" cables are hauled diagonally backwards. The progress of the "haul" is carefully with the dancer's head throughout its execution. This action represents the ship's anchor being dragged up from the sea.

Cairngorm — The brooch which attaches a dancer's plaid to the shoulder (National Dress) contains a cairngorm stone, which is a yellow or smoky-brown variety of crystalline quartz, found in the Cairngorm mountain range in North-East Scotland.

Caithness — Highland Games, usually held the first Saturday in July.

Cake Walk — A stage dance for a lady and a gent, developed from walking steps and figures, consisting mainly of a high prance with a backward tilt. See S.O.H.D.A. Dance Sheet No. 34.

the a.b.c of highland dancing and games directory

Caledonian Club of San Francisco — Highland Games, usually held the first weekend in September in California, U.S.A.

Calf — The fleshy part of the leg behind and below the knee — where the working foot is vertically placed in 3rd Rear Aerial Position.

Calgary — Highland Games, usually held the third Saturday in July in Alberta, Canada.

Callander — Highland Games, usually held the fourth Saturday in July.

Cambridge — Highland Games, usually held the third Saturday in July in Ontario, Canada.

Campbell — Highland Games, usually held the third Saturday in August in California, U.S.A.

Campbeltown — Highland Games, usually held the third Saturday in June.

Canmore — Highland Games, usually held the first Sunday in September in Alberta, Canada.

Caol (Fort William) — Highland Games, usually held the first Saturday in August.

Capitol District — Highland Games, usually held the first Saturday in September in New York, U.S.A.

Carriage — This covers the general appearance of the dancer. IE, especially concerning the use of hands, arms, head, etc. See Deportment.

Carrick — Lowland Games, usually held the first Sunday in June.

Casting (Arm action in "Sailors' Hornpipe") — As the working foot is extended, stretch both arms down directly towards it. As the working foot is brought in, bring both arms up across the body to represent the effect of casting over the dancer's shoulder on the opposite side.

Central Coast — Highland Games, usually held the first Saturday in May in California, U.S.A.

Central New York — Scottish Games, usually held the second Saturday in August in New York, U.S.A.

Centre Crossing ("Sword Dance") — is where the blade of the sword crosses the scabbard.

Ceres — Highland Games, usually held the fourth Saturday in June.

Certificate — A document issued by an organisation certifying that one has satisfactorily completed a course of studies or has passed a qualifying examination and has attained a specific standing in a given field.

the a.b.c of highland dancing and games directory

Change — A motion of specified height started on the balls of both feet, with the body weight equally distributed, in 3rd or 5th Position, and ended at the same time on the balls of both feet in 3rd or 5th Position with a change of the working foot.

Charleston — Highland Games, usually held the third Saturday in September in South Carolina, U.S.A.

Chassé — A gliding step in dancing. Glide the working foot forward, close the other foot to 3rd Rear or 5th Rear position and glide the working foot forward again.

Chevrolet Celtic Classic — Highland Games, usually held the fourth weekend in September in Pennsylvania, U.S.A.

Chicago — Scottish Festival, usually held the third Saturday in October in Illinois, U.S.A.

Chirnside — Highland Games, usually held the third Sunday in May.

Chord (Played by accordionists, fiddlers, etc.) — A series of notes played together at the start and finish of a tune, during which the bow or curtsey should be executed.

Circle — The name given to the 1st Step of the "Sailors' Hornpipe." In the days of the old sailing ships, when a crewman danced a hornpipe on board the ship's narrow decks, he always started the performance by describing a wide circle among his fellow crew members in order to "make room" for his remaining steps! (See also "Clearing The Decks").

City of Newtown — Highland Games, usually held the second Monday in March in Victoria, Australia.

Clansman Sword Dance — A dance, conceived in Australia, for 4 dancers (2 ladies + 2 gents) which commences in Strathspey tempo with the 4 dancers carrying swords, which are eventually placed on the ground as in the "Argyll Broadswords." Eight steps are then executed, in, over and around the swords.

Clap — As a signal for the piper to change from slow to a faster tempo, the dancer must clap hands on the last beat of the slow step.

Claremore — Highland Festival, usually held the third Saturday in April in Oklahoma, U.S.A.

Clarkston — Highland Games, usually held the second Sunday in June.

Claymore (from Gaelic *claidheamh mòr* — a broad sword) — A large two-edged sword. Four claymores, or basket-hilted Broadswords, are the traditional swords used when performing the Broadswords.

Clearing the Decks — Name often given to the 1st Step of "Sailors' Hornpipe." The action of the circle executed during this step was, in fact, a method of making a clear space on the ship's deck in order to perform the remaining steps of the dance.

Clenched Fist (Arm movement in "The Irish Jig") — As "Irish Jig" is supposedly performed by an "angry" Irishwoman, the shaking of the clenched fists can regularly be observed by both male and female dancers.

Climbing the Riggin' (Grasping Rungs) — An arm action in the "Sailors' Hornpipe" where one hand is lifted above head height, grasps the rope ladder rungs and lowers to chest with a little roll of the body.

Clinging the Riggin' (Grasping The Sides) — An arm action in the "Sailors' Hornpipe" where one hand is lifted with a relaxed elbow above head height, grasps the rope ladder sides and lowers to the side of the chest with a little roll of the body.

Clip-Heels (Movement in "Irish Jig") — Raise the R leg at the side with straight or bent knee and good turn-out. Hop on the LF and strike the heels together during the elevation, finishing with a straight leg.

Close — Term used to describe a coming together of the working foot to the supporting foot. This movement is used during a Hop and Travel, Travel Balance movement, Seven Step Side Travel, etc.

Closed Position — occurs when both feet touch each other, or the working foot makes contact with the supporting leg..

Coatbridge — Highland Games, usually held the fourth Sunday in August.

Cobourg — Highland Games, usually held the first Saturday in July in Ontario, Canada.

Collingwood — Scottish Festival and Tattoo, usually held the first Saturday in July in Ontario, Canada.

Colonial — Highland Games, usually held the third Saturday in May in Delaware, U.S.A.

Competition (Indoor or Outdoor) — A contest in friendly rivalry between dancers of various age groups and standards for rewards.

Competition Convener — A representative of a dancing organisation elected annually to organise and arrange all aspects of Highland Dancing competitions — indoors and outdoors. It is the competition convener's task to verify dates, times, groups, etc., of each competition and arrange adjudicators, pipers, stewards, etc., for each venue.

the a.b.c of highland dancing and games directory

Connecticut — Scottish Festival, usually held the first Saturday in October in Connecticut, U.S.A.

Consolation — An extra event organised usually at the end of a competition for dancers who have been unsuccessful in the regular events.

Contra — The other side. IE, to dance a movement contra is to repeat the movement on the opposite foot.

Co-Ordination — The dancer should ensure that his or her handwork and armwork coincides exactly in time with the footwork during a performance.

Cortachy — Highland Games, usually held the third Sunday in August.

Costa Mesa — Highland Games, usually held the last weekend in May in California, U.S.A.

Count — To take into account the number of beats, bars, measures, etc., of music, and so give a uniform tempo during the performing of a dance.

Coupé — Term used in Scottish Country Dancing. The same as a Balance in Highland Dancing.

Cowdenbeath — Highland Games, usually held the fourth Saturday in June.

Crab Walk (Movement in "Sailors' Hornpipe") — Start with a spring forward to land in 1st Inverted Position Flat, then turn on the heel of RF and the ball of LF into 1st Position Flat (Count 1 and). Turn on the ball of RF and the heel of LF into 1st Inverted Position Flat then turn on the heel of RF and the ball of LF into 1st Position Flat (Count 2 and). Repeat as required. See also "Forward Crab Walk."

Cramp Roll (Movement in "The Irish Jig") — Spring or Shuffle (this Tap motion can be left out) on to ball of RF. With feet parallel, beat ball of LF. Beat R heel, then L heel (Count and 1 and a 2).

Crieff — Highland Games, usually held the third Saturday in August.

Crossed Position — is one in which the working foot crosses over the supporting foot in a specified position. IE., 3rd Crossed Position.

Cupar — Highland Games, usually held the first Sunday in July.

Curtsey — A gesture of respect. A movement executed by the female dancer to signify the start and finish of Hebridean or National dances — equivalent to Bow (men).

D

Dallas — Highland Games, usually held the first Saturday in September in Texas, U.S.A.

Dance — A dance is a joining together of a number of basic steps.

Dancer's Delight — A solo Highland dance of 6 steps in 2/4 March tempo. It was conceived and developed in January 1964 to commemorate the First Anniversary of the United States Highland Dancers' Association (USHDA). It is purely an exhibition dance and should not be executed competitively. See S.O.H.D.A. Dance Sheet No. 32.

Daylesford — Highland Games, usually held the first weekend in December in Victoria, Australia.

Dedication — Every dancer must seek to maintain a constant level of devotion by giving one's whole interest in achieving the highest standard of perfection in the art of Highland Dancing.

Delco — Highland Games, usually held the third Saturday in June in Pennsylvania, U.S.A.

Demi-Plié (Movement used in the dance "Scotch Measure") — Assemble with the RF in 5th Position, with a slight bending of both knees.

Demi-Plié and Turn (Movement used in the dance "Scotch Measure") — Dance a demi-plié as described above (Count 1). Disassemble on to the LF, extending the RF out to 2nd Aerial Position (Count 2). Making one complete turn on the spot to the right, dance a bourrée on the RF (Count and 3, and 4).

Deportment — This covers interpretation (the ability of the dancer to express the spirit and motif of the dance), balance, general appearance and comportment, thus embracing carriage of the head, body, arms and hands.

Detroit — Highland Games, usually held the first Saturday in August in Michigan, U.S.A.

Development (Développé) — The act or process of expansion of movements during dancing.

Diagonal — A direction equally spaced between front and side. IE, at 45 degrees to the Line of Direction.

Dingwall — Highland Games, usually held the second Saturday in July.

Direction — is the line on which steps are taken. Besides the obvious directions like right, left, forward and backward, in between these lines are directions like right front diagonal (RFD), left front diagonal (LFD), right back diagonal (RBD), left back diagonal (LBD), etc.

Disassemble — A motion of specified height started on the balls of both feet in a closed position with the body weight equally distributed, and ended on the ball of one foot with the working foot placed in a precise position.

Displace — When the working foot takes the place of the supporting foot to move it to another position, the working foot is said to displace the supporting foot.

Donnybrook — Name given to a rather energetic step in the "Irish Jig." With the shaking of fists/shillelagh and the angry fervour and character of the dance, the step takes its name from a riotous fair held many years ago in the district of Donnybrook, Dublin.

Double Shuffle (Movement in "Sailors' Hornpipe") — On RF — Beat the ball of the LF and execute a shuffle with the RF (C. 1 and a). Beat the ball of the RF in 3rd Position, beat the ball of the LF in 3rd Rear Position, and shuffle with the RF (C. and 2 and a).

Double Swords — Although not so well known in the Northern Hemisphere, the "Double Swords" is regularly performed on dancing programmes in the Southern Hemisphere. It consists of more or less the original "Sword Dance," but performed by two dancers, working as a team, who start and finish the slow and quick tempos at Swords 2 and 4. It was thought that as the usual solo "Sword Dance" took up so much time at venues when performed by dozens of competitors in each age group, the idea of "doubling up" — two dancers to each sword — halved the performance time, and added variety to the usual steps with the slight variations needed to avoid the dancers coming in contact with each other's feet, knees, etc. The "Double Swords" has now grown into a precise art form, making it an outstanding spectacle at any dancing venue. A time-saver all round — especially for the over-worked piper, who only has to play "half" of his original programme!

Doublet — A close-fitting sleeved or sleeveless jacket worn by Highland Dancers. The doublet is usually made of velvet and edged with silver or gold braid.

Double Treble (Movement used in "The Earl of Errol" and "The King of Sweden") — Dance a Single Treble as described (Count 1 and and a 2 and and); Beat ball of LF in 3rd Position, and beat ball of RF in 3rd Rear Position (Count a 3). Execute a small outward brush with the LF out to 4th Intermediate Aerial Low Position, followed with a small inward brush with the LF to 3rd Aerial Low Position, then again beat ball of LF in 3rd Position and beat ball of RF in 3rd Rear Position (Count and and a 4). Repeat on opposite foot or as required. See "Single Treble."

Douglas, Jenny — The first-ever woman to compete in the all-male Highland Dancing events at Games. In the late 19th century, she appeared in the same outfit as the men — bonnet, plaid, sporran, etc. — and at that time caused shock waves throughout the Highland Dancing world!

Dornoch — Highland Games, usually held the first Friday in August.

Drop (Movement used in "The Irish Jig") — Similar to a Spring, but landed stronger. Can also be executed on the flat of the foot.

Drumnadrochit — Highland Games, usually held the fourth Saturday in August.

Drumtochty — Highland Games, usually held the fourth Saturday in June.

Duet — A dance performed by two dancers. IE, "Lochaber Swords," "Double Swords," "Cake Walk," etc.

Dufftown — Highland Games, usually held the fourth Saturday in July.

Dunbeath — Highland Games, usually held the third Friday in July.

Dundee — Highland Games, usually held the first Sunday in July.

Dundonald — Highland Games, usually held the first Saturday in August.

Dunedin — Highland Games, usually held the second Saturday in April in Florida, U.S.A.

Dunfermline — Highland Games, usually held the fourth Saturday in July.

Dunoon (Cowal) — Highland Games, usually held the fourth Friday and Saturday in August.

Durness — Highland Games, usually held the fourth Friday in July.

Dusty Miller — A solo Hebridean Dance of 6 steps in 6/4 tempo — count 6 beats to the bar. See S.O.H.D.A. Dance Sheet No. 8.

Dutton — Highland Games, usually held the second Saturday in June in Ontario, Canada.

E

Earl of Erroll — A Highland solo step dance of 6 steps for boy or girl in 4/4 tempo, composed in the mid-eighteenth century by Francis Peacock (1723 — 1807), an Aberdeenshire dancing master. See S.O.H.D.A. Dance Sheet No. 16.

Eastern Cape — Highland Games, usually held the second Saturday in April in South Africa.

East Lothian — Highland Games, usually held the fourth Sunday in August at Meadowmill.

Eastwood — International Highland Games, usually held the first Sunday in June.

Echt — Highland Games, usually held the second Saturday in July.

Elevation — Height a dancer should strive to attain throughout a dance, with a hop or spring.

Elgin — Highland Games, usually held the first Saturday in July.

Entrechât — A motion of specified height started on the balls of both feet in 3rd or 5th Position. On take-off both legs are crossed from back to front, and kept as close together as possible. The dancer lands on the balls of both feet in the original starting position.

Entry Form — A list of details to be completed in order that the competitor may compete in a future competition. Most entry forms must be completed and returned to the organiser or promoter by a specified date.

Examinations — A number of tests of capacity and knowledge the dancer endeavours to successfully pass, either physically, orally or by written hand, during his/her training life, the ultimate accomplishment being the achievement of full Teacher's status.

Examining Convener — A representative of a dancing organisation elected annually to organise and arrange all aspects of Highland Dancing examinations from Primary to Full Teacher status. It is the examining convener's task to organise venues, adjudicators, pipers, etc., and also arrange for medals, trophies, certificates, etc., to be allotted for eventual presentation to the successful candidates. An annual financial statement should also be available for the following Examiners A.G.M.

Execute — To carry out a movement in dancing.

Execution — Standard of ability performed by the dancer.

Extend — When the working foot is extended, it is stretched out, away from the supporting leg, to a specified open position.

F

Falkirk— Highland Games, usually held the third Sunday in June.

Farewell (Arm action in "Sailors' Hornpipe") — Short for "May you fare and prosper well." With R arm placed in 1st Position, the R arm (during Counts 1, 2) is raised at the side in a circular motion. The R arm (on Count 3) is brought in to the head level. IE, representing the waving of a flag. This action was reproduced from the sailor of yesteryear as he waved farewell to his loved ones from the deck of his ship. The step was once danced waving a little Union Jack which was concealed in the tunic sleeve.

Feet — The two most important components of the human body for Highland Dancers. It is essential that care is taken to look after these "tools of your trade!" At the first sign of any irregularity, E.G., pain, inflammation, redness, swelling, etc., medical advice must be found.

Fergus — Highland Games, usually held the second weekend in August in Ontario, Canada.

Festival — An indoor or outdoor annual dancing competition covering two or three days over a weekend. Its theme usually commemorates the anniversary of a notable historical event or figure.

Fettercairn — Highland Games, usually held the first Saturday in July.

Figure of Eight — Although not depicting the actual shape of a figure 8, the expression is the name often given to the direction of travel the four dancers follow while executing the Progressive Strathspey and Progressive Reel movements of the "Strathspey and Highland Reel." The term more accurately fits the pattern cut by three dancers dancing a "Reel of Three." Thus, the modern "Strathspey and Highland Reel" would more accurately be called a "Reel of Four" which it is, also it is just one of many ways of "reeling" within the Scottish dance tradition. The oldest reference to a definite "Reel of Three" is found in 1710 and "Reels of Four" have been known since 1776.

Figures — A series of steps or movements in a dance.

Finger Grouping — In all arm positions of Highland Dancing, except 1st Position, the fingers are simply spaced and the thumb touches the first joint of the middle finger.

First of August — A solo Hebridean hornpipe in 2/4 tempo. It is rather different from the other Hebridean step dances, being a tap-dance a little reminiscent of the "Earl of Erroll" or an Irish Hornpipe. See S.O.H.D.A. Dance Sheet No. 27.

Fisherman's Jersey — A roll-neck woollen jersey, worn by the dancer as part of the original costume while performing "The First of August."

Flap (Movement in "The Irish Jig") — On RF: Begin the movement by lifting the RF in front of the body — can also start in 2nd Inverted Aerial Position. Dance a forceful tap step, using a slack leg motion, to end taking the weight on the flat of the R foot, the LF raised at the back with a slight knee bend.

Flashes — A bright garter or ribbon worn to support the hose, when wearing the Highland Dress, a small portion of ribbon showing below the hose turnover.

Flat Position — is one in which the whole of one or both feet are flat on the ground, and turned out at a specified angle.

Flickers — A movement executed by the dancer during certain steps of "The First of August." It is reminiscent of the "Charleston" step of the 1920s.

Flicking the Coat-Tails (Arm movement by the male dancer in "The Irish Jig") — While the working hand is raised and executing a twirling movement with the shillelagh, the other hand is tucked under the tail-coat on that side, back of hand against the body, and a flicking action with the fingers is executed in tempo with the music.

Flinging — See "Shedding."

Flora MacDonald — Highland Games, usually held the first Saturday in October in North Carolina, U.S.A.

Flora MacDonald's Fancy — A solo Hebridean step dance in slow 6/8 Jig tempo, traditionally for girls. This dance was presumably conceived some years after the 1745 rebellion as a tribute to Flora MacDonald (1722-1790). It has been passed down over the years from generation to generation, and it is thanks to Isobel Cramb, an Aberdeenshire dancing mistress, for the 6 steps we know today. See S.O.H.D.A. Dance Sheet No. 12.

Flowers of Edinburgh — A Scottish solo step dance of six steps in 2/4 tempo. Thanks are due to Jack McConachie for the description of the six steps we know today. See S.O.H.D.A. Dance Sheet No. 7.

Folded (Second arm position in "Sailors' Hornpipe") — The folded arms are positioned away from the body with the fingers straight and the palms facing down. The fingers on the back of the R hand touch the L arm close to the elbow joint, while the fingers on the back of the L hand and the back of the L wrist touch the R forearm — so the "tarry" palms do not come in touch with the tunic sleeves.

Follow Through — With the RF in 4th Intermediate Aerial Position, spring on to the RF, displacing the LF up to 3rd Rear Aerial Position (Count 1). Pass the LF, as in shedding, to 3rd Aerial Position (Count and). Hopping on the RF, extend the LF out to the 4th Intermediate Aerial Position (Count 2).

This movement is sometimes called "Round-the-leg" as in "Balance & Round-the-leg."

Foot Positions — There are 5 basic foot positions used by the Highland Dancer. Each basic foot position is measured from the Line of Direction (See Line of Direction). The 5 basic foot positions are described as follows -

- **1st Position** — The weight of the body is equally distributed, with the heels touching. Both feet form an angle of 90 degrees and each foot is turned out at an angle of 45 degrees from the Line of Direction.
- **2nd Position** — With the toe and heel of the working foot in alignment with the heel of the supporting foot, the leg of the working foot is extended to the side at an angle of 90 degrees from the Line of Direction.
- **3rd Position** — The working foot is in contact with the instep cavity of the supporting foot, on the toe, half-point, heel or ball. The working foot is placed at an angle of 90 degrees from the Line of Direction.
- **4th Position** — The working leg is turned out at an angle of 45 degrees from the Line of Direction, as the working foot is extended forward with both heels in alignment with the Line of Direction.
- **5th Position** — The working foot touches the big toe of the supporting foot, both feet turned out an angle of 45 degrees from the Line of Direction.

Forfar — Highland Games, usually held the second Sunday in June.

Forres — Highland Games, usually held the second Saturday in July.

Fort Erie — See "Loch Sloy."

Fort William — See Lochaber.

Forward Crab Walk (Movement in "Sailors' Hornpipe") — With the LF in 5th Inverted Position Flat, turn the LF outwards on the L heel, toes inclined upwards (Count 1). Dance a Ball-Dig with the RF in 3rd Rear Position (Count and). Repeat with the opposite foot on the other side (Count 2 and). Repeat as required.

Forward Crossing Turn — This is the term used mainly by Highland Dancers in the Southern Hemisphere for the turning movement executed during Bar 4 of the Pointing Step in the "Sword Dance." IE, L toe pointed in D in 2nd Pos (C. 5). Quarter turn to left pointing L toe in 3rd or 5th Pos (C. 6). R toe pointed in 2nd Pos in B (C. 7). R toe pointed in 3rd or 5th Pos (C. 8).

Foursome — A dance performed by four dancers, preferably two male and two female. IE, "Hullachan," "Strathspey/Reel," "Broadswords," "Irish Reel," etc.

Fresno — Highland Games, usually held the third Saturday in September in California, U.S.A.

G

Galashiels — Highland Games, usually held the first Saturday in July.

Galloway — See Garnock.

Garnock — Highland Games, usually held the fourth Saturday in May.

Gathering In (An arm action in "Sailors' Hornpipe") — A sequence of pulling motions with interchanging arms, representing the rolling up of the ship's tarry ropes. This action should be executed with both arms slightly below the level of the waistline.

Georgetown — Highland Games, usually held the third Saturday in June in Ontario, Canada.

Georgina — Highland Games, usually held the third Saturday in June in Ontario, Canada.

Gillie Callum — The title of the tune played on the bagpipes for the present-day solo "Sword Dance." At some Northern Games the dance is called by the name "Gillie Callum."

Glasgow — Highland Games, usually held the first weekend in June in Kentucky, U.S.A.

Glenfinnan — Highland Games, usually held the third Saturday in August.

Glengarry — Highland Games, usually held the second Saturday in July.

Glengarry — Highland Games, usually held the fourth Saturday in July in Ontario, Canada.

Glenisla — Highland Games, usually held the third Friday in August.

Glenluce — Highland Games, usually held the first Saturday in August.

Glenrothes — Highland Games, usually held the fourth Sunday in July.

Glenurquhart — See Drumnadrochit.

Glissade — A movement of two small gliding steps, the second quickly following behind the first, usually sideways or forwards.

Gourock — Highland Games, usually held the second Sunday in May.

Grace — Both male and female dancers should strive to attain a manner of easy elegance of form while executing a dance.

Grades — The stages of promotion a Highland Dancer obtains through the advancement of periodical examinations.

Grandfather Mountain — Highland Games, usually held the first weekend after July 4th (Independence Day) in North Carolina, U.S.A.

Grange — Highland Games, usually held the fourth Sunday in June.

Grantown-on-Spey — Highland Games, usually held the fourth Sunday in June.

Great Smoky Mountains — Highland Games, usually held the third weekend in May in Tennessee, U.S.A.

Grind (Movement in "The Irish Jig") — 4 Beat: With the working foot placed in 5th Position or 4th Opposite 5th Position, dance two heavily-stressed Ball-Changes from the ball of the supporting foot to the ball of the working foot (Count 1 and a 2).

3 Beat: Execute the first three beats of the 4-Beat definition.

Ground Position — occurs when both feet are touching the ground.

H

Half-Cutting — A movement, usually in Strathspey tempo, used by dancers in the Southern Hemisphere during the "Highland Fling." With the RF in 3rd aerial position, slide the RF down the front of the L leg, spring on to the RF, sliding the LF up the back of the R leg to 3rd rear aerial position (Count 1). Slide the LF down the back of the R leg, spring on to the LF, sliding the RF up the front of the L leg to 3rd aerial position (Count 2). Repeat counts 1, 2 (Count 3, 4).

Half-Point — When the first two or three pads of the working toes are touching the ground, with the ball of the foot well off the ground, it is said to be placed on the half-point.

Haliburton — Highland Games, usually held the second Saturday in July in Ontario, Canada.

Halkirk — Highland Games, usually held the fourth Saturday in July.

Hamilton — Highland Games, usually held on Hogmanay (December 31) in Hamilton, South Island, New Zealand.

Hands on Back (Arm movement in "Sailors' Hornpipe") — An arm action where one or both hands are placed on the small of the back, palms facing outwards. Used during Crab Walk in Circle step, where one hand is placed in this position, while the other is raised to 4th (Lookout) Arm Position.

Harris — Gala Day and Games, usually held the fourth Saturday in July.

Hastings — Highland Games, usually held the third weekend in April in Hastings, North Island, New Zealand.

Hauling (An arm action in "Sailors' Hornpipe") — With both arms at waist level, reach them forward diagonally with open fingers towards the same side as the working foot (Count 1). While closing the fingers and with a pulling motion, bring both arms inwards and across the dancer's body at the level of the waist (Count 2).

Head Positions — In Highland Dancing there are two head positions. In the 1st Position the head faces the front and the eyes are level. In the 2nd Position the head is directed diagonally to the left or right (away from the working arm).

Hebridean — Pertaining to the area where many of the National Dances originated.

Hebridean Dances — Traditional dances that were devised, a few centuries ago, throughout the Western Isles of Scotland. As opposed to Highland Dances, which were conceived over the centuries throughout the Scottish mainland.

Hebridean Laddie — A solo Hebridean dance of 6 steps in 2/4 Reel tempo. Reputed to be an early version of "Highland Laddie." See S.O.H.D.A. Dance Sheet No. 33.

Heel — The working foot is said to be placed on the heel when it touches the ground, the sole of the foot upright and straight.

Heel-Beat (Movement in "The Irish Jig") — Similar to a Heel-Tap except that the working heel ends on the ground.

Heel-Change (Movement in "The Irish Jig") — Similar to a Ball-Change, except that the change of weight is from the working heel to the ball of the supporting foot.

Heel-Clip (Movement in "The Irish Jig") — With the RF positioned on the ball, the heel of the LF comes in contact with the R heel as the LF travels forward through 1st Position.

Heel-Dig (Movement in "The Irish Jig") —Maintaining an upturned slant of the working foot, smartly hit the heel of the working foot in a specified position.

Heel-Hit (Movement in "The Irish Jig") — Using the Shillelagh, the male dancer strikes the heel of the Irish Jig shoe of the raised leg.

Heel Position — is one which is taken on the heel of the working foot, using a straight or relaxed knee.

Heel-Roll (Movement in "Sailors' Hornpipe") — With both feet placed close to each other and with the toes upturned, travel rearwards, with both knees relaxed, dancing a sequence of Heel-Digs.

Heel-Tap (Movement in "Sailors' Hornpipe") — On RF: With the R knee relaxed and the ball of the RF in a specified position, and with the R heel lifted high off the ground, smartly hit the R heel on then off the ground.

Heel-Toe (Occupying 2 beats of music) — Hop on the LF, place the R heel in 2nd Position (Count 1). Hop on the LF, and point the R Toe in 5th Position (Count 2). Repeat as required.

Helmsdale — Highland Games, usually held the third Saturday in August.

High-Cut — Spring onto the LF and, on landing, place the RF in 3rd Rear Aerial Position (Count 1). (The RF may or may not be extended to 2nd Aerial Position during the elevation.) Smartly re-extend the RF out towards 2nd Aerial Position and quickly bring it back to 3rd Rear Aerial Position (Count and). Repeat on opposite foot and as required.

High-Cut in Front — As for the High-Cut description, but the working foot is placed in 3rd Aerial Position (Count 1 and):

Highland Dress — The National Dress of Scotland, including kilt, plaid, sporran, etc.

Highland Fling — A traditional Scottish solo step dance, performed without travel, in 4/4 Strathspey tempo. Legend has it that it was inspired by the sight of a stag curvetting in the distance — hence the raised arms representing the stag's antlers. Another tale states that it was originally danced on a targe or shield and this presumably accounts for the precise stepping on the spot. See S.O.H.D.A. Dance Sheet No. 4.

Highland Games — Competitive meetings held throughout the year where the skills and techniques of various Scottish athletic sports (including Highland Dancing) are contested.

Highland Laddie — A Scottish solo step dance of 6 steps in 2/4 tempo — although some early manuscripts describe 8 steps. See S.O.H.D.A. Dance Sheet No. 1.

Highland Reel — This dance usually follows the Strathspey, with the music changing to Reel time without any break between the dances. See S.O.H.D.A. Dance Sheet No. 22.

Highlands and Islands Association — Highland Games, usually held the first Saturday in October in Missouri, U.S.A.

Highland Schottische — A setting movement, occupying 2 bars of music in Strathspey tempo, and commonly used in Scottish Country Dancing and throughout the semi-Highland threesome "The Shepherd's Crook" as follows:

Hop on the LF, point the R toe in 2nd Position (Count 1); Hop on the LF, place the RF in 3rd Rear Aerial Position (Count 2); Hop on the LF, point the R toe in 2nd Position (Count 3); Hop on the LF, place the RF in 3rd Aerial Position (Count 4); Step RF towards 2nd Position (Count 5); Close the LF to 3rd Rear Position on the balls of both feet (Count 6); Step the RF towards 2nd Position (Count 7); Spring on to the RF and place the LF in 3rd Rear Aerial Position (Count 8). Repeat on the opposite foot and as required.

Highland Society — A body or organisation whose members are interested in upholding the traditions of the songs, dances and the written word of everything that is Scottish.

Hilt — The handle of the sword. "The Sword Dance" starts and finishes at the hilt.

Hip — The head of the thigh bone. The dancer must maintain firm hip control while performing, ensuring a good turn-out of both thighs and maintaining both knees are out fully at each side.

Hitching (Third arm position in "Sailors' Hornpipe") — With both arms (fingers stretched) at waist level, one hand touches the middle of the body with palms facing down and thumb underneath, the other hand is placed at the rear at waist level, back of hand against the body.

Hitch-Kick (Movement in "The Irish Jig") — Beginning with one foot at the rear, bring it forward up to 4th Aerial Position, spring onto it and kick the opposite foot high in front.

H. & N.D.A. (Highland and National Dancers of Australia) — An organisation originated in 1931 in Victoria, Australia, whose aim is to maintain and encourage the art of Highland Dancing and to promote competitions and displays and to retain the traditional steps handed down by the Dancing Masters from Scotland.

Hoisting Slacks (Arm movement in "Sailors' Hornpipe") — Assemble with the RF in 3rd position (Count 1) — during this count both arms are stretched out to the sides then placed in 3rd (Hitching) Position (R arm in front).

the a.b.c of highland dancing and games directory

Disassemble on to the LF, and shake the RF out to 2nd Forward Aerial Position (Count 2) — during this count the slacks (trousers) are hitched upwards.

Honolulu — Highland Games, usually held the first Saturday in April in Hawaii, U.S.A.

Hooch! — Though rarely heard nowadays, the dancers of yesteryear were often heard to shout their delight at set dances (Reels, Broadswords, etc.), by emanating cries of wild fervour while performing, in order to excite and invigorate the other members of the dance team.

Hop — is a motion of specified height started on the ball of one foot and ended by landing on the ball of the same foot.

Hop and Travel — Hop on the LF and extend the RF towards 4th Intermediate Aerial Position then bend the R knee to bring the RF approximately halfway between 3rd Aerial Position and 4th Intermediate Aerial Position on landing (Count 1). Step the RF on half-point to 4th Intermediate Position, closing the ball of the LF to take the weight in 5th Rear Position, and extending the RF out to 4th Intermediate Aerial Position (Count and 2).

Hop, Brush, Beat, Beat (on RF) — With the RF extended out to 4th Intermediate Aerial Position, hop on the LF and brush the RF in to 3rd Aerial Low Position (Count 1 and); Beat the ball of the RF on half-point in 3rd or 5th Position then lightly beat the LF in 3rd or 5th Rear Position, extending the RF out to 4th Intermediate Aerial Position (Count a 2). Repeat as required.

Hose — Stockings, which should match the tartan of the kilt as part of the Highland Dress.

Hopetoun Reel — A dance for 4 dancers (2 ladies, 2 gents) starting in slow tempo and changing to a faster tempo. This dance was devised in Australia by a group of dancing teachers in honour of the first Governor General — Lord Hopetoun — during his term in office.

Houston — Highland Games, usually held the last Saturday in April in Texas, U.S.A.

Hullachan — See Reel of Tulloch.

Huntly — Highland Games, usually held the fourth Saturday in June.

Huntly Fling (The Marquis of Huntly's Highland Fling) — A solo Highland dance of 8 steps in 4/4 Strathspey tempo, devised in 1841, and an early version of the "Highland Fling." See S.O.H.D.A. Dance Sheet No. 6.

I

Illinois — St Andrew's Society Highland Games, usually held the third Saturday in June In Illinois, U.S.A.

Imperfect Half-Beat Rhythm — In the 1st Step of the "Sword Dance," the Pas de Basque movement (on RF) is counted as: Land on RF (C. 1), close LF immediately to RF (C. and), beat RF (C. 2). The first two movements are done almost simultaneously and counted as "1 & 2." (See Perfect Half-Beat Rhythm).

I.S.T.D. (The Imperial Society of Teachers of Dancing) — Although not a "specialist" Highland Dancing Association, the I.S.T.D. do have, amongst other branches of dance, a Highland Branch which organises examination and teacher certificate tests in Highland and National Dances.

Indiana — Highland Games, usually held the third Saturday in July in Indiana, U.S.A.

Instep — The prominent arched part of the foot. IE, Where the working foot in placed in 3rd Position.

Interlaced (Fifth arm position in "Sailors' Hornpipe") — Both arms are extended straight down in front of the body, palms facing downwards, with the fingers of both hands interlaced.

Intermediate — Term used to categorise the advancement of a dancer from the stage of "Novice."

Intermediate Position — occurs when the working foot is placed halfway between 2nd and 4th Positions, either on the ground, in the air or to the rear.

Introduction — A number of bars of music, sometimes 4 or 8, played at the start of a dance, during which a bow or curtsey is executed. The introduction also gives the dancer an indication of the tempo of the music that is to follow. Usually there is a 4-bar introduction to Strathspeys and an 8-bar introduction to Reels and Jigs.

Inveraray — Highland Games, usually held the third Tuesday in July.

Invercharron — Highland Games, usually held the third Saturday in September.

Invergarry — See Glengarry.

Invergordon — Highland Games, usually held the fourth Saturday in August.

Inverkeithing — Highland Games, usually held the first Saturday in August.

Inverness — Highland Games, usually held the third Saturday in July.

Inverted Position — occurs when the working foot and/or both feet are turned into a specified position with the heel/s pushed forward.

Inward Brush — On RF: The RF softly comes in contact with the ground as it travels from an open aerial position to a specific closed position.

Irish Hornpipe — A dance of 8 steps performed in New Zealand in 2/4 tempo. It is executed in the manner of Irish Dancing and involves a lot of shuffles and beatings in a steady rhythm.

Irish Jig — A Scottish Character dance and is performed at Highland Games and competitions throughout Scotland and is not a traditional Irish dance. See S.O.H.D.A. Dance Sheet No. 30.

Irish Jig (Double time) — A dance of 8 steps in 6/8 time. Performed in New Zealand in a character and style like the real Irish Dancing. The dance contains characteristic Breaks, Grinding, Triples, etc. In Double Time the bar usually consists of six quavers in two triplets and the dance is performed in a slower tempo compared with the Single Time Jig. The Double Time Jig incorporates simple rhythm, pauses and intermediate beatings between the time beats.

Irish Jig (Single time) — A dance of 8 steps in 6/8 time. Performed in New Zealand in a character and style like the real Irish Dancing. The dance contains characteristic Breaks, Grinding, Triples, etc. The Single Time signifies a simple rhythm, using either pauses or 6 beats to each bar of music, these movements all performed on the music counts.

Irish Reel — A dance for 4 persons, executing intricate beating and shuffle steps with figures in between. It consists of 9 parts in 4/4 Slow Reel tempo. It's a dance performed in New Zealand.

Irvine — Highland Games, usually held the third Tuesday in July.

Isle of Mull — Children's Highland Games, usually held the first Wednesday in July.

J

Jabot — A frill of lace worn in front of a woman's dress or on a man's shirt front as part of the Highland Dress.

Jackson — Highland Games, usually held the first Saturday in November in Mississippi, U.S.A.

Jacksonville — Highland Games, usually held the second Saturday in April in Florida, U.S.A.

Jack Tar (Arm movement in "Sailors' Hornpipe") — An arm action performed from 2nd Folded Arm Position, slapping the thighs with a downward and backward movement, indicating wiping the tar off the hands.

Jacky Tar — Another title for the dance known today as the "Sailors' Hornpipe." At some Northern Games, the dance is still called by the name "Jacky Tar," so called because the duties of the sailor in bygone days caused his hands and clothes to be tarred by the ship's tackling.

Jakarta — Highland Games, usually held the first Sunday in June in Jakarta, Indonesia.

Jewellery — It is advisable that all dancers should not over-burden themselves with unnecessary ornamentation of any type, IE, loose or dangling jewellery. The only items of adornment permissible are a wedding ring and in essential cases a medicare bracelet.

Jig — A lively dance tempo, which is the oldest form of dance music surviving, is found in three forms: the "single jig" (in 6/8 and occasionally in 12/8 time); the "double jig" (in 6/8 time); and the "hop" or "slip jig" (in 9/8 time). The word "Jig" undoubtedly derives from the Italian word "giga."

Jig Shoes — A leather dancing sandal with a hard sole and heel, worn as part of the "Irish Jig" costume. The uppers are usually leather of various shades — red and green being the most common. The chrome leather shaped base sole consists of a strong cowhide sole with an extra-hard vulcanised tip. The all-leather blocked heel contains a cast brass plate into which is fitted a jingle tap.

Johannesburg — Caledonian Games, usually held the third Saturday in May in Johannesburg, South Africa.

Jump — A motion of specified height started with the dancer's weight on one or both feet and ended by alighting at the same time in a specified position on both feet.

K

Kansas City — Highland Games, usually held the first weekend in June in Kansas, U.S.A.

Keith — Highland Games, usually held the first Sunday in August.

Kelso — Highland Games, usually held the first Saturday in July.

Kenmore — Highland Games, usually held the first Wednesday in July.

Kentucky — Scottish Weekend, usually held the second weekend in May in Louisville, Kentucky, U.S.A.

Kilbirnie — See Garnock.

Kilchoan — Highland Games, usually held the third Friday in July.

Kilmore & Kilbride — Highland Games, usually held the first Saturday in June.

Kilt — A man's short pleated skirt of tartan, forming part of the Highland Dress.

Kilt Pin — An item of jewellery worn as an adornment on the lower corner of the kilt apron. It is often in the shape of an eagle's claw or Celtic-shaped silver pin.

King of Sweden — A solo step dance of 6 steps and chorus in 4/4 tempo. It is very similar in technique to the "Earl of Erroll." Both contain a good deal of Double Trebling and would appear to have been composed about the same time — the mid-eighteenth century. See S.O.H.D.A. Dance Sheet No. 26.

Kinloch Rannoch — Highland Games, usually held the third Saturday in August.

Knee — The joint above the shin bone. The dancer must ensure that no position or movement in Highland Dancing should be executed above the level of the knee.

Knee-Cap — The movable bone covering the front of the knee-joint. The kilt should hang to approximately 2 inches (5 cm) above the centre of the knee-cap.

Knee Slap — A movement performed during the "Sailors' Hornpipe" and the "Irish Jig," where the hand slaps the working knee, which is raised to approximately waist height.

L

Laces — A length of thin cord used for fastening dancing shoes. It is to the dancer's benefit that all laces be knotted securely, double knotted, and the ends and loops tucked away out of sight.

Lady Louisa MacDonald of Sleat — A Scottish solo step dance of 6 steps in 6/8 tempo. It is but one of a few dances collected by Mary Isdale MacNab of Vancouver, Canada. See S.O.H.D.A. Dance Sheet No. 20.

Lanark — Highland Games, usually held the second Thursday in June.

Landing — From a hop or a spring, when the supporting foot alights on the ground, the term used is — Landing on the LF ...

Langholm — Highland Games, usually held the fourth Saturday in July.

Lateral Coupé (Side-cut) — Circle RF through 2nd Low Aerial Position to spring on to it in 5th Rear Position, displacing the LF out to 2nd Low Aerial Position (Count 1).

Leap — A motion of specified height started on the balls of both feet in 5th Position. On take-off both legs are extended at equal height towards 2nd Aerial position. The movement is ended by alighting on the balls of both feet at the same time, with or without a new working foot in front.

Leg-Warmers — A pair of thick, woollen, footless "stockings" covering the ankles up to the thighs and worn by the dancer during rehearsal and class time. The object is to keep the muscles in the legs warm and supple while the dancer is not performing and so help prevent strains and muscle tightening.

Leotard — A skin-tight garment worn for class practice, rehearsals, etc., by dancers. It can be long-sleeved or sleeveless, legs varying from none at all to ankle length and was devised by the 19th century trapeze artiste Jules Léotard.

Lesmahagow — Highland Games, usually held the third Saturday in June.

Lesson Time — Dancers must ensure that time set aside for dancing classes is for that specific purpose and is for almost every week of the year. Other interests must never intrude on your dancing class time.

Lewis — Highland Games, usually held the fourth Saturday in July.

Ligonier — Highland Games, usually held the second Saturday in September in Pennsylvania, U.S.A.

Limber-Up (Warm-Up) — A preparatory set of exercises performed by every dancer to warm and tone up the muscles in preparation for the physical effort of dancing that is to follow.

Line of Direction — is a supposed line drawn on the ground from which all the basic foot positions are measured. It travels between the heels of the dancer from back to front while placed in 1st Position Flat.

Line Set — When standing in a straight line in preparation for dances such as "Strathspey and Highland Reel" or "Strathspey and Reel of Tulloch," the 4 dancers are said to be taking formation in a Line Set. (See Rectangular Set).

Linking of Arms — The palms of each dancers hand gently supports his partners arm just slightly above the elbow. The thumb should not encompass the upper arm, as this is simply an assistance to maintain balance and not a "clutch." Each dancers forearm lies parallel alongside that of his partner.

Lochaber — Highland Games, usually held the fourth Saturday in July.

Lochaber Broadswords — A Sword Dance for 4 dancers in Reel tempo. The 5 steps are performed over 4 Broadswords, points touching in a "+" formation. The dance might have originated out of the Argyll Broadswords, but is today considered as a dance of its own. See S.O.H.D.A. Dance Sheet No. 24.

Lochaber Swords — A dance for 2 dancers, in Strathspey and Reel tempo, over one set of crossed swords. The original dance was supposed to have been conceived while Prince Charles Edward Stuart, after landing at Moidart, was raising the standard at Glenfinnan.

Lochcarron — Highland Games, usually held the third Saturday in July.

Lochearnhead — Highland Games, usually held the fourth Saturday in July.

Lochinver — Highland Games, usually held the second Friday in August.

Loch Prado — Highland Games, usually held the third weekend in October in California, U.S.A.

Loch Sloy — Highland Games, usually held the first Sunday in July in Ontario, Canada.

Lonach — Highland Games, usually held the fourth Saturday in August.

Lone Star — Highland Games, usually held the second Saturday in October in Texas, U.S.A.

Long Island — Scottish Games, usually held the fourth Saturday in August in New York, U.S.A.

Long's Peak — Scottish Festival, usually held the second weekend in September in Colorado, U.S.A.

Look-Out *Shading* (Fourth arm position in "Sailors' Hornpipe") — With the L hand placed in 1st Position, the R hand is lifted, with fingers stretched and palms down, close to the forehead. The R thumb touches the R index finger, and the R elbow faces to the side with a straight forearm.

Loon Mountain — Highland Games, usually held the third Saturday in September in Massachusetts, U.S.A.

Lorn — Show and Sports usually held the first Saturday in August.

Lourin Fair (Old Rayne) — Highland Games, usually held the third Saturday in August.

Low-Cutting (Movement in "Sailors' Hornpipe") — Prepare with the LF extended out in 2nd Aerial Low Position and with a hop on the RF with a slight travel to the right, strike the the instep of the LF against the R heel then smartly extend the LF once again out to 2nd Aerial Low Position (Count and). Strike the instep of the LF against the R heel again, at the same time springing on to the LF, which displaces the RF smartly out to 2nd Aerial Low Position (Count a 1). This motion is repeated to the opposite side and as required. Low-Cutting is meant to represent the sailor sliding on a slippery deck!

Luss — Highland Games, usually held the third Wednesday in July.

M

MacNeil of Barra — A dance from the collection of Mrs. Mary Isdale MacNab, late of Vancouver, Canada, arranged for 1 gent and 6 ladies, occupying 48 bars in Strathspey tempo and 64 bars in Reel tempo. The slow tempo is made up mainly of the ladies dancing round MacNeil (the gent), who performs "Highland Fling" type steps. The Reel tempo consists of the ladies dancing setting and turning and reels of three across and diagonal with MacNeil, who also does some Reel setting steps and High Cutting in the centre.

Maine — Highland Games, usually held the third Saturday in August in Maine, U.S.A.

Make-Up — This should be kept to a basic minimum. On no account should the dancer's face be transformed with any sort of false fabrication in the hope of supplementing their facial appeal!

Mallaig & Morar — Highland Games, usually held the first Monday in August.

Manitoba — Highland Games, usually held the first Saturday in July in Manitoba, Canada.

March — A piece of music for marching. Is commonly in duple time, 2/4 or 6/8 for quick march. Many Reels and Jigs are also known to Pipers as Marches and it is commonplace that a "March"-setting of a Reel or a Jig is used for dances such as "Highland Laddie," "Miss Forbes," "Flora MacDonald's Fancy," and so forth.

Marin County — Highland Games, usually held the second Saturday in May in California, U.S.A.

Markinch— Highland Games, usually held the first Sunday in June.

Massachusetts — Highland Games, usually held the third Saturday in June in Massachusetts, U.S.A.

McHenry — Highland Festival, usually held the first Saturday in June in Maryland, U.S.A.

Meadowmill— See East Lothian.

Medal— A reward in the shape of a metal disc given to successful competitors who have attained premier placings in dancing competitions. IE, Usually gold for first place, silver for second place and bronze for third place.

Metro — Highland Games, usually held the first weekend in July in Nova Scotia, Canada.

Mey— Highland Games, usually held the second Saturday in August.

Midway Turn(Danced during "turn" at 1st Step of "Sword Dance") —

> Bar 2: With a 1/4 turn to the right, dance a Pas de Basque on the RF at Corner A (Count 5and 6). With a 1/2 to the right on the spot, dance a Pas de Basque on the LF (Count 7and 8).

Milwaukee — Highland Games, usually held the first Saturday in June in Wisconsin, U.S.A.

Miss Forbes — A girl's solo Highland dance of 5 steps in 2/4 tempo. See S.O.H.D.A. Dance Sheet No. 25.

Missoula — Scottish Games, usually held the second Saturday in August in Montana, U.S.A.

Modesta — Highland Games, usually held the first Saturday in June in California, U.S.A.

Molson — Highland Games, usually held the fourth Saturday in July in Ontario, Canada.

Monifieth — Lowland Games, usually held the third Sunday in July.

Monklands — Highland Games, usually held the first Sunday in June.

Monterey — Highland Games, usually held the first Saturday in August in California, U.S.A.

Montreal — Highland Games, usually held the first weekend in August in Quebec, Canada.

Montrose — Highland Games, usually held the third Sunday in August.

Montrose Doublet — This is a double-breasted doublet with a closed front. It is styled with a stand-up collar and has a diagonal row of silver buttons on each side from shoulder to waist with 3 silver buttons in a vertical line on each sleeve. It is worn with a black belt and silver ornamental buckle. The lower edge of the doublet may be masked by the belt or may show slightly below. A lace jabot must be worn with the Montrose doublet.

Morar — See Mallaig.

Movement — The act of changing a position or posture.

Muffler — A scarf of red or Paisley material casually worn round the neck of the male dancer as part of the "Irish Jig" outfit.

Mull — Children's Highland Games, usually held the first Wednesday in July.

Muscle Cramps — These spasms may occur while performing a dance or much later after the physical activity. It could be due to an insufficient blood flow or lack of body salt due to perspiration. The best remedy is to slowly stretch the affected muscle while putting firm pressure on it through a gentle kneading action. Walking gently on the affected leg or foot often helps to break the muscle tension.

Music — The art of expression in sound.

N

Nairn — Highland Games, usually held the second Saturday in August.

Nashville — Highland Games, usually held the first weekend in October in Tennessee, U.S.A.

Natal — Scottish Games, usually held the first Saturday in April in Natal, South Africa.

Natal South Coast — Highland Games, usually held the fourth Saturday in May in Natal, South Africa.

National Outfit— Worn by female dancers during the performing of the Scottish National dances and consisting of blouse, velvet scalloped tunic, and tartan circular skirt over underskirts — See Aboyne Dress.

Nethybridge — Highland Games, usually held the third Saturday in August.

New Brunswick — Highland Games, usually held the last weekend in June in New Brunswick, Canada.

Newburgh — Highland Games, usually held the third Saturday in June.

New Deer — Highland Games, usually held the third Saturday in July.

New Hampshire — Highland Games, usually held the third weekend in September in Lincoln, New Hampshire, U.S.A.

New Jersey — Scottish Festival, usually held the first Sunday in October in New Jersey, U.S.A.

New South Wales — Highland Games, usually held the first Sunday in October in New South Wales, Australia.

Newtonmore — Highland Games, usually held the first Saturday in August.

New Zealand Academy of Highland and National Dancing (Inc.) — Established in 1946 the Academy is an examination organisation whose objects, amongst others, are to foster and encourage under the auspices of the Piping and Dancing Association of New Zealand (Inc.) Highland and National dancing in New Zealand, ... to foster correct and recognised techniques in the same .. and promote the interests of members of the Academy and to advance the art of Highland and National dancing in its traditional form.

Norcross — Scottish Fair, usually held the second Saturday in October in Georgia, U.S.A.

North Lanark — Highland Games, usually held the fourth Saturday in August in Ontario, Canada.

North Uist — Highland Games, usually held the third Saturday in July.

Novice — Term used to categorise the advancement of a dancer from the stage of "Beginner."

O

Oban — See Argyllshire Gathering.

Oberlin — Highland Games, usually held the fourth weekend in June in Ohio, U.S.A.

Ohio — Highland Games, usually held the fourth Saturday in June in Ohio, U.S.A.

Oklahoma — Highland Games, usually held the third Saturday in September in Oklahoma, U.S.A.

Old Meldrum — Highland Games, usually held the third Saturday in June.

Old Rayne (Lourin Fair) — Highland Games, usually held the third Saturday in August.

Open — Term used to categorise the advancement of a dancer from the stage of "Intermediate."

Open Pas de Basque — Similar to the Pas de Basque movement, except that the working foot is placed in 4th Opposite 5th Position, and no extension of the working foot is executed at the finish.

Open Position — occurs when the working foot is placed away from the supporting foot or leg.

Oral Theory — Used during certain medal tests and advanced examinations where the entrant replies in words to the questions of the examiner.

Orak Shrine — Highland Games, usually held the fourth Saturday in August in Indiana, U.S.A.

Orlando — Highland Games, usually held the last weekend in January in Florida, U.S.A.

Outward Brush — On RF: The RF softly comes in contact with the ground as it travels from a rear or specified closed position, through 1st Position, to an open aerial position.

Overstep — A step or spring, when the working foot crosses over the supporting foot, taking the weight.

Over the Water to Charlie — A solo Hebridean dance of 6 steps in 6/8 Jig tempo, for men. The title of the dance actually comes from a toast given by the loyal followers of Bonnie Prince Charlie. It appears that when the English conquerors raised their glasses to the King, the Scots would inconspicuously pass their glasses over a fingerbowl or any such liquid on the table and reply, "To the King (who is over the water!")".

This, of course, was in praise of Bonnie Prince Charlie, the man in their eyes who should have been King, but, as we all know, had to flee "over the water" to France and safety. See S.O.H.D.A. Dance Sheet No. 3.

Ozark — Scottish Festival, usually held the second weekend in April in Arkansas, U.S.A.

P

Pacific — Highland Games, usually held the first weekend in October in California, U.S.A.

Pacific North-West — Highland Games, usually held the last weekend in July in Washington, U.S.A.

Paisley — International Highland Games, usually held the second Saturday in June.

Palmerston North — Highland Games, usually held the second Saturday in December in Palmerston North, North Island, New Zealand.

Parallel Position — is an elevated position where both feet are extended an equal distance. IE, Leap, etc.

Parallel Springs — Name given by dancers from the Southern Hemisphere for what is known here as Leaps (See Leaps).

Pas de Basque — With the RF extended out to 2nd medium Aerial Position, spring on to the RF, landing the LF on half-point in 3rd or 5th Position (Count 1and); Beat the ball of the RF in 5th Rear Position, simultaneously extending the LF in preparation for the next movement (Count 2).

This movement can be danced with or without extension.

Pas de Basque — Counting (2 Pas de Basques) for :

Strathspey tempo: 1 & 2 3 & 4 = (1 bar) (Perfect or Even half-beat rhythm).

Reel tempo: 1 & 2 3 & 4 = (2 bars) (Perfect or Even half-beat rhythm).

"Sword Dance": 1& 2 3& 4 = (1 bar) (Imperfect half-beat rhythm).

Pas de Basque Derrière — Similar to Pas de Basque movement, but instead of landing the working foot in 3rd or 5th Position, it is placed in 5th Rear Position, and on the initial spring there is a forward diagonal travel to 4th or 4th Intermediate Position.

Passing Through Position — A position of arms or feet which cannot be held for a time count.

the a.b.c of highland dancing and games directory

Pattern — is the shape of the dance or performance. It is made by the movement of the dancer or dancers as they execute varying steps in different directions on the dance platform or stage.

Payson — Highland Games, usually held the second Saturday in July in Utah, U.S.A.

Peebles — Highland Games, usually held the fourth Saturday in June.

Penalise — When a dancer makes a mistake or touches his sword during competition, he is penalised by the adjudicator who deducts points depending on the severity of the offence.

Pensacola — Highland Games, usually held the second Saturday in November in Florida, U.S.A.

Perfect Half-Beat Rhythm — In the "Shean Triubhais," Reels and National Dances, the Pas de Basque movement (on RF) is counted as: Land on RF (C. 1), close LF to RF (C. and), beat RF (C. 2), and is equally counted as "1 and 2." (See Imperfect Half-Beat Rhythm).

Perth — Highland Games, usually held the second Sunday in August.

Peterhead — Highland Games, usually held the fourth Saturday in July.

Petticoat — Worn under the tartan taffeta skirt of the ladies National outfit — full, white and fairly plain — as part of the National costume.

Philadelphia/South Jersey — Annual indoor Highland Dancing competition, usually held the first Saturday in November in Pennsylvania, U.S.A.

Pike's Peak — Highland Games, usually held the third Saturday in July in Colorado, U.S.A.

Piper — Musician who plays the Scottish bagpipes. May accompany Highland Dancing.

Pitlochry — Highland Games, usually held the second Saturday in September.

Pivot Turn (Turning to the left) — Cross the RF over the LF in 3rd Crossed Position, at the same time starting to spin to the left on the ball of the LF. Without any displacement, continue spinning on the balls of both feet to end facing the front with the LF in 3rd or 5th Position.

Placing the Swords — In placing the sword on the dancing platform in order to perform the "Sword Dance," the scabbard opening is placed to the left with the blade placed over the scabbard, making four equal quarters.

Plaid — A long piece of woollen cloth, usually tartan, worn over the shoulder as part of the Highland Dress. IE, Left shoulder for men, right shoulder for women.

Plié — A movement in dancing in which the knees are bent while the body remains upright.

Plié and Turn (Movement used in "Scotch Measure") — Assemble in a demi-plié (both knees bent) with the RF in 5th Position (Count 1). Disassemble on to the LF, extending the RF out to 2nd Aerial Position (Count 2). Hop on the LF, then Bourrée Derrière with the RF, making one complete turn on the spot to the right (Count and 3 and 4).

Point — When the tips of the first two toes are in contact with the ground, and with the instep arched, the foot is said to be pointed.

Point Position — A position where the big toe is in contact with the floor.

Poise — The composure a dancer must attain to achieve perfect carriage and balance to the body.

Polka — A movement consisting of one hop and three steps using 4th Position, 5th Rear Position and 4th Ball Positions passing through 1st Position (Count and 1 and 2). May be preceded by a brush forward (Count and a 1 and 2).

Portland — Highland Games, usually held the third Saturday in July in Oregon, U.S.A.

Portree — Highland Games, usually held the first Wednesday in August.

Pose — An artistic position, posture or attitude often struck at the end of a dance (E.G., "Highland Laddie") or performance.

Positions — Any of the postures of the feet, head and arms on which all steps and movements in Highland Dancing are based.

Practise — In order that a Highland Dancer may acquire and maintain skills in the art, regular and habitual exercise must be observed to preserve a high standard.

Pre-Open Section — Before attaining the status of Open Dancer, which allows the dancer to enter events open to all dancers, the young enthusiast enters and progresses through the Pre-Open Sections of competitions, comprising Baby, Beginners, Novice and Intermediate. The rules of most dancing organisations usually require the entrant to gain a certain number of "First" prizes in one section before advancing upwards to the next section.

Prince Charlie Coatee — This is a dress jacket worn by the male dancer. It is styled with revers and collar and cut away at the front and features a short tail at the back with 2 upright tabs each ornamented with 3 silver buttons in a vertical line, There is a silver button at the lower edge of each side of the centre back. Each sleeve has an upright tab with 3 silver buttons in a vertical line. There is a tab on each shoulder with a silver button at the neck edge.

Propelled Pivot Turn (To the right) — With a slight spring on to the RF, the partners link R arms (See Linking of Arms) — L arm in 2nd Position (Count 1). They now place the LF on half-point in 2nd Position and compensate for a small movement of the RF (Count and 2). The turn is completed by repeating the movements related for the "and 2" counts as often as required.

Progressive Reel Movement — On RF: Hop on the LF and, with a slight right shoulder lead, place the RF in 3rd Aerial Position (Count and). Step the RF along the Line of Travel to 4th Intermediate Position (Count 1); Close the LF to 5th Rear Position (Count and) and step with the RF along the Line of Travel (Count 2). Repeat with LF and as required.

Progressive Strathspey Movement — On RF: With the RF placed in 3rd Aerial Position and, with a slight right shoulder lead, step the RF along the Line of Travel to 4th Intermediate Position (Count 1); Close the LF to 5th Rear Position, extending the RF out to 4th Intermediate Aerial Position (Count 2). Facing the Line of Travel, spring on to the RF, placing the LF in 3rd Rear Aerial Position (Count 3). Hop on the RF and, with a slight left shoulder lead, pass the LF, as in shedding, to 3rd Aerial Position (Count 4). Repeat with LF and as required.

Puirt-a-Beul (Gaelic Mouth Music) — An early form of vocal accompaniment for dancers, still used today for television, stage and display purposes.

Pulling Ropes (Arm action in "Sailors' Hornpipe") — With R arm: Extend the R arm straight up with open fingers, then pull the R arm with closed fingers smartly down to below the level of the waist. This action can also be executed to the front, the working arm stretched outwards and travelling parallel with the ground in towards the body, below the level of the waist.

Pumping (Arm action in "Sailors' Hornpipe") — While performing a low knee-bend, extend both hands (fists clenched) down below the level of the waist (Count 1). While regaining the original upright state, bring both hands (still clenched) up to shoulder height, with both elbows pointed at the sides and the shoulders pulled straight back (Count 2).

Pumps — A soft-soled sandal, made of leather, worn as part of the Highland Dancing costume, the flexibility of the sandal enabling the dancer to attain a good point of the toe.

Pupil — One who has been taught or influenced by a teacher.

Pushing Up or Down of Sleeves — An arm action commonly used by dancers from the Southern Hemisphere during the "Sailors' Hornpipe." One arm is placed in front of the body at a slight angle with the palm facing down. Using the other hand, grip the sleeve of the tunic at the wrist and push the sleeve up, using the thumb and forefinger, to the elbow.

Repeat the action in reverse for the pulling-down motion. If the sleeves are pushed up at the commencement of each half step, they must be pulled down at the end of each half step.

Q

Quarter-Beat Rhythm — A musical term where the counting of a movement is broken into 4 beats of equal value in the space of time occupied by one beat and counted as "1 and and a." E.G., used during Single and Double Trebles.

Queechee — Scottish Festival, usually held the third Saturday in August in Queechee, Vermont, U.S.A.

Quick Steps — A combination of short rapid dance steps.

Quick Time — Steps, usually performed at the end of a dance and executed at a faster tempo, are said to be done in quick time. The commencement of quick time is signalled by a clap of the hands as an indication to the accompanist to alter the tempo of the music.

R

Rear — Any position or movement executed behind the supporting foot is said to be done to the rear.

Rear Position — occurs when the working foot is placed in a specified position to the rear of the supporting foot.

Rectangular Set — When standing in a rectangular shape (a dancer at each corner) in preparation for the "Reel of Tulloch" of "Hullachan," the four dancers are said to be taking formation in a Rectangular Set (see Line Set).

Reel — See Highland Reel.

Reeling — is the name given when all dancers are performing the Figure of Eight movement during the "Strathspey and Highland Reel."

Reel of Tulloch (Hullachan) — This dance usually follows the Strathspey as an alternative to the "Highland Reel." It is said to have originated on a wintry Sunday at the small village of Tulloch, near Ballater, in Aberdeenshire, in 1780.

the a.b.c of highland dancing and games directory

While waiting for the minister to arrive, the congregation, standing in the aisles, started to dance reel steps and swing each other by the arms, in order to keep warm. Thus the "Reel of Tulloch" was conceived and in today's version very little of the character and spirit of that bygone day has been lost. See S.O.H.D.A. Dance Sheet No. 22.

Renaissance — Highland Games, usually held the first weekend in October in California, U.S.A.

Retiré — Skips forward or backwards, maintaining a good turn-out.

Rhythm — The periodic or uniform emphasis in music.

Rio Grande Valley — Celtic Festival and Highland Games, usually held the third Saturday in May in New Mexico, U.S.A.

Rise — A rising on the balls of the feet, keeping the knees straight.

River Grove — Scottish Fair, usually held the third Saturday in October in Illinois, U.S.A.

Rocking — Spring on to the RF, point the L toe in 3rd Rear Position (Count 1). Spring on to the LF, point the R toe in 3rd or 5th Position (Count 2). The rear foot is always the first to be pointed.

Rocking (Movement in "Sailors' Hornpipe") — On RF: With the RF placed a little forward of 5th Position, roll on to the inside edge of the RF and the outside edge of the LF (Count 1). Roll both feet in the other direction, IE., the outside edge of the RF and the inside edge of the LF (Count 2). Repeat as required..

Rocky Mountain — Highland Games, usually held the second weekend in August in Colorado, U.S.A.

Rosin — A translucent pale yellow crystal that is rubbed over the sole of dancing shoes in order to prevent slipping on polished surfaces.

Rosneath & Clynder — Highland Games, usually held the third Sunday in July.

Ross — Highland Games, usually held the second Saturday in March in Ross, Tasmania.

Rothiemurchus — Highland Games, usually held the fourth Sunday in July.

Round Hill — Highland Games, usually held on July 4th (Independence Day) in Connecticut, U.S.A.

Round the Leg (Or Shedding Movement) — See Shedding.

Roybridge — Friendly Games, usually held the third Saturday in July.

Russian Bourrée (Movement in "The Village Maid") — The motion comprises three small steps on the balls of the feet, executed diagonally. With the LF flat on the ground with a slightly bent knee, extend the RF with straight knee to 4th Aerial Position (Count and); Step the RF forward to 4th Position (Count 1); Close the LF to 5th Rear Position and again step the RF forward to 4th Position (Count and 2). Repeat on opposite foot and as required.

S

Sacramento — Highland Games, usually held the third weekend in April in California, U.S.A.

Sailors' Hat — Worn as part of the outfit for "Sailors' Hornpipe." The hat should be white, the cap tally being black with gold lettering. The hat is worn forward on the forehead, resting 2 finger-widths above the eyebrows.

Sailors' Hornpipe — A solo dance performed at most competitions and Highland Games, depicting the movements and daily routines of a sailor on board a ship. See S.O.H.D.A. Dance Sheet No. 31.

Salado — Highland Games, usually held the first weekend in November in Texas, U.S.A.

Salutation —Opening and closing "bow" used constantly by dancers from Australia. The opening and closing salutation is executed by stepping backwards with the RF from 1st Position into 4th Rear Position, pointing the L toe into 3rd Position (bending slightly from the waist) and then stepping forward with the LF to 4th Position and closing the RF to 1st Position flat. At the end of all dances, step back into bow from the position the dance is concluded in, do not return to 1st Position first, dropping hands to the sides when stepping forward into 1st Position.

Salute (Arm movement in "Sailors' Hornpipe") — With the feet and head in 1st Position and arms extended down at the sides, the R arm is raised upwards and the hand is smartly taken inwards, palm facing down and thumb folded under first finger, which is placed against the forehead slightly above the right eyebrow. After a short hesitation, the R arm is smartly dropped straight down to end in the original starting position.

San Diego — Highland Games, usually held the third Saturday in June in California, U.S.A.

Santa Rosa — Highland Games, usually held the first weekend in September in California, U.S.A.

Sarnia — Highland Games, usually held the third Saturday in August in Ontario, Canada.

Savannah — Highland Games, usually held the first Saturday in May in Georgia, U.S.A.

Scabbard — A leather or metal sheath of a sword.

Schottische — A dance, or dance tune, similar to the polka. This setting movement, occupying one bar of music in Strathspey tempo, is commonly used in Scottish Country Dancing and in the semi-Highland threesome "The Shepherd's Crook," as follows on RF.

> Step the RF towards 2nd Position (Count 1); Close the LF to 3rd Rear Position on the balls of both feet (Count 2); Step the RF towards 2nd Position (Count 3); Springing on to RF, place the LF in 3rd Rear (Low) Aerial Position (Count 4). Repeat on the opposite foot and as required.

Scissors (Movement in "Sailors' Hornpipe") — With the weight on the balls of both feet, turn the L heel outwards, with both knees inwards, and lift the RF at the side with the R heel tilted up and out (Count 1). Turn both heels in and, with the knees turned out, place the RF in 5th Position (Count and). Repeat on opposite foot and as required..

Scotch Measure — A twa-some dance of 6 steps (and break) in 2/4 march tempo for boy and girl. During the twa-some version a 16-bar break can be included after the 1st and 6th step, making the steps up to 8. It can also be performed as a solo dance of 6 steps. The dance was found in the Hill Manuscript dated 1841 and was studied and collected by Aberdeenshire dancing mistress Isobel Cramb. See S.O.H.D.A. Dance Sheet No.14.

Scotchtown — Scottish Festival and Games, usually held the third weekend in May in Virginia, U.S.A.

S.D.T.A. (Scottish Dance Teachers' Alliance) — Although not a "specialist" Highland Dancing Association, the S.D.T.A. do have, amongst other branches of dance, a Highland Branch which organises examination and teacher certificate tests in Highland and National Dances.

Scott's Settlement — Scottish Festival, usually held the first Saturday in September in Ohio, U.S.A.

Scottish Lilt — A girl's solo traditional dance of 8 steps in 9/8 tempo (Count 3 beats to the bar). The dance is supposed to have been composed after 1746 in Perthshire and has been handed down through the years from teacher to teacher. See S.O.H.D.A. Dance Sheet No.10.

Seil Island — Highland Games, usually held the fourth Saturday in June.

Selkirk — Highland Games, usually held the third Saturday in June.

Seminar — A group of advanced students working in a specific subject under a teacher — a class at which a group of students discuss a particular topic.

the a.b.c of highland dancing and games directory

Sertoma — Highland Games, usually held the fourth Saturday in May in Ontario, Canada.

Set Dance — A dance that is performed by more than one dancer, IE, "Reel of Tulloch," "Broadswords," etc.

Setting Step — A series of movements executed by two dancers facing each other. During the "Strathspey, Reel and Reel of Tulloch" various steps occupying 8 bars of music are performed by the dancers between each Progressive Strathspey and Progressive Reel movements and before each swinging movement of the "Reel of Tulloch."

Seven Step Side Travel — Hopping on the LF, step the RF in 5th Rear Position (Count and 1); Take six little steps sideways to the left on the balls of the feet, LF, RF, LF, RF, LF, RF. Each time the RF is placed in 5th Rear Position and the LF towards 2nd Position (Count and 2 and 3 and 4). This movement can also be performed with a weaving action — the RF landing in 5th Rear Position and 5th Position alternately.

Shake — A shake is a movement performed with or without a hop, where the working foot is extended, with a good turn-out, to an open aerial position. Flex the working knee slightly and re-extend to the original open aerial position.

Shake Shake Down — Hop on the LF, execute a shake with the RF in 4th Intermediate Aerial Position (Count 1). Hop on the LF, execute a shake with the RF in 2nd Aerial Position (Count and); Spring the RF in to 5th Rear Position to displace the LF out to a required position (Count 2). Both shakes (Count 1 and) can be executed in 2nd Aerial Position.

Shaking of Fists/Shillelagh — During the "Irish Jig," especially the "break," and as the dance is supposedly being performed by a "mad" Irishwoman, the girl dancer continually shakes one or both fists to show anger. The male dancer does much the same by shaking the shillelagh in the same manner.

Shar — In most parts of the Southern Hemisphere the movement Shar — IE, Shar on RF — is exactly the same was what is known elsewhere as a Hop, Brush, Beat, Beat on RF, and counted as "1 and a 2."

Shean Triubhais — (*Seann Triubhas* - Gaelic for old trews or trousers) — A graceful solo Highland Dance which starts slowly and increases in tempo on the final two steps. After the defeat of Bonnie Prince Charlie at Culloden, in 1746, by the Duke of Cumberland, it was decreed that the kilt be denounced and trews be worn instead. The slow tempo of the "Shean Triubhais" is said to depict the disgust at the wearing of the trews and the quick steps are a display of pleasure in their abolition when the Act was repealed in 1782. See S.O.H.D.A. Dance Sheet No. 9.

Shedding — The name given to a movement used continuously throughout the dance "Highland Fling," where the working foot is passed from 3rd Rear Aerial Position to 3rd Aerial Position and back to 3rd Rear Aerial Position, keeping the working foot close to the supporting leg throughout the movement and the knee pressed well back. The apron of the kilt should be "flat."

Shellman — Highland Games, usually held the third weekend in November in Georgia, U.S.A.

Shepherd's Crook — Actually classed as a Scottish Country dance in 4/4 Strathspey tempo, for one gent and two ladies, this threesome is made up mainly of Schottisches, Highland Schottisches and "Highland Fling" steps throughout.

Shillelagh — A prop. used by the male dancer throughout the "Irish Jig." It is a cudgel-shaped sapling cut from an oak or blackthorn, and so called from a village of the same name in County Wicklow.

Shillelagh Twirling — A hand movement continuously used by the male dancer during the "Irish Jig." With a twisting wrist action the shillelagh appears to turn continuously in a steady circle in the dancer's raised right hand.

Shin — Front of the leg, below the knee — where the working foot is placed in 3rd Aerial Position.

Shin Splint — This complaint produces pain to the front of the shin when weight is taken on the ball of the foot. The pain usually intensifies after activity and does not respond to heat or therapy. The primary cause could be performing on a rock-hard unyielding surface and a doctor should be consulted immediately.

Shotts — Highland Games, usually held the first Saturday in June.

Shoulder Lead (R and L) — While executing a Progressive Strathspey Movement or Progressive Reel Movement in the "Strathspey and Highland Reel," with both arms raised in 3rd Position, all dancers must ensure while "passing" the other members of the set that the shoulders are turned 1/8 of a turn to right or left to avoid colliding with each other! This shoulder lead is attained by a slight "twist" of the waist.

Shriner's — Scottish Games, usually held in mid-July in Massachusetts, U.S.A.

Shuffle — With the RF extended out to mid-4th Aerial Position, spring on to the RF extending the LF out to mid-4th Aerial Position. Brush the LF in to 5th Position and smartly out to mid-4th Aerial Position (Count 1and). Repeat on opposite foot and as required.

Shuffle (Tap movement used in "Sailors' Hornpipe" and "Irish Jig") — A small outward brush quickly followed by a small inward brush.

Shuffle Over the Buckle — Name given to the 2nd Step of the "Sailors' Hornpipe," where the Shuffle movements are executed at an angle over the top of the foot, or where the sailor of yesteryear wore a buckle to fasten his shoes.

Side and Forward Crossing — This is the term used mainly by Highland Dancers in the Southern Hemisphere for the "pointing" movement executed during Bars 2 and 3 of the Pointing Step in the "Sword Dance." IE, Bar 2; L toe pointed in D in 2nd Position (Count 5). L toe pointed in 3rd or 5th Position (Count 6). L toe pointed in B in 4th Position (Count 7). L toe pointed in 3rd or 5th Position (Count 8). Bar 3: Repeat Bar 2 movement on opposite foot (Count 1, 2, 3, 4).

Side Travel — A side travel movement using closed and open ball positions in a series. Closed positions are taken on the Time counts, while open positions are executed on the "and" counts.

Single-Beat Rhythm — A musical term where the counting of a movement in stated simply as 1, 2, 3, 4. EG, Shedding, Rocking, Spring Points, Outwards Brushes, etc.

Single Shuffle (Movement in "Sailors' Hornpipe") — On RF — Beat the ball of the LF and execute a shuffle with the RF (Count 1 and a).

Single Treble (Movement in "The Earl of Erroll") — Hop on the LF, extend the RF out to 4th Intermediate Aerial Position (Count 1); Brush the RF inwards to 3rd Aerial Low Position then step on it in 3rd Position (Count and and), small outward brush with LF towards 4th Intermediate Aerial Low Position, followed by a small inward brush on LF to 3rd Aerial Low Position (Count a 2), step the ball of the LF in 3rd Position then gently beat the ball of the RF in 3rd Rear Position (Count and and). Repeat on opposite foot and as required.

Skean Dhu (Gaelic **Sgian:** Knife, **Dubh:** Black) — A small ornamental dagger or knife displayed in the right stocking of the male Highland Dancer as part of the Highland Dress. Is worn if desired.

Skip Change of Step — The method used in Scottish Country Dancing of executing a Progressive Reel Movement. IE, Without placing the working foot in 3rd Aerial Position on the initial hop.

Slap (Movement in "The Irish Jig") — On RF: With the R leg lifted to the front with bent knee, smartly strike the RF down flat on the ground, lifting the LF at the back with a slightly bent knee.

the a.b.c of highland dancing and games directory

Sleeve Ruffles — A ribbon of fine lace worn by the male dancer round each wrist and protruding slightly below each cuff, when wearing the Montrose doublet, and may be worn in conjunction with the lace jabot as part of the Montrose Highland Dancing outfit.

Slide — A form of music tempo and also a form of dance practised in Ireland.

Slip Jig — The term for a 9/8 Jig in Irish Dancing is generally a "Slip Jig," (or "Hop Jig"). The only solo Highland Dance in 9/8 time is the "Scottish Lilt."

Socks ("Irish Jig") — While executing the "Irish Jig," young girl dancers are advised to wear knee-length socks in red, green or white. Older girls may wear tights in red, green or natural.

S.O.B.H.D. (The Scottish Official Board of Highland Dancing) — was brought about in the 1950s with the intention of, among other things, standardising the steps of the various Highland Dances. The S.O.B.H.D. help organise the dancing events at various Highland Games and competitions and, although most of the events are advertised as "Open/Premier," they are restricted to their own registered members. Any member found entering a non-S.O.B.H.D. "approved" event will be banned from further S.O.B.H.D. venues for a specified period!

S.O.H.D.A. (Scottish Official Highland Dancing Association) — Founded in 1947 by prominent dancers and teachers of that time, the S.O.H.D.A. was formed to encourage the art of Highland Dancing by promoting competitions, examinations, seminars and holding meetings to discuss with parents, teachers and dancers the views and history of our Highland and National dances and their music.

Sole — The underside of the foot.

Solo — A performance of a dance, etc., done by one person.

South Canterbury — Caledonian Games, usually held on January 1 (New Year's Day) in South Island, New Zealand.

South-East Florida — Scottish Festival, usually held the first Saturday in March in Florida, U.S.A.

Southend — Highland Games, usually held the fourth Saturday in July.

South Maryland — Highland Games, usually held the fourth Saturday in April in Maryland, U.S.A.

South Uist — Highland Games, usually held the third Wednesday in July.

Splay Foot — In the dancing world, to be splay-footed (both feet turned outwards) can be advantageous to the performer, as all basic foot positions are taken from the Line of Direction with a well-turned-out supporting and working foot.

the a.b.c of highland dancing and games directory

Spokane — Scottish Festival, usually held the fourth Saturday in July in Washington, U.S.A.

Sporran — An ornamental pouch worn by the male Highland Dancer on the front of the kilt as part of the Highland Dress. By wearing the kilt, and so lacking trouser pockets, the Highlander of yesteryear had his sporran instead. It descended from the simple bag, closed with draw-strings, that was attached to the belt of every mediaeval traveller. In due course, this developed a fold-over top, and with the disappearance of the belted plaid had to be slung on its own strap, which now hung loose around the hips. From this came the modern hide sporran with its tooled design on the flap and swinging tassels to the bag.

Sprains — Usually involves mishaps to the ligaments and joints. The symptoms are pain, bruising and often swelling and medical advice may be required to ensure there are no bone fractures.

Spring — A motion of specified height started on the ball of one foot and ended by landing on the ball of the opposite foot.

Spring Kick (Movement in "Sailors' Hornpipe" and "The Irish Jig") — Similar to Hitch-kick. With the LF on the ground, spring on to the RF, kicking the LF high to the front.

Spring Point — Spring on to the RF and, point the L toe in a specified position, landing both feet on the ground at the same time (Count 1). Repeat on opposite foot and as required.

Staff — Musical notes are written on or in the five horizontal parallel lines and four spaces of the musical staff.

Stamp (Movement in "The Irish Jig") — A forceful beat with the sole of the foot on the ground.

St. Andrews — Highland Games, usually held the fourth Sunday in July.

St. Fillan's Society Games — The first-ever meeting, held in Perthshire in 1819, that could truly be called "Games," as it was the first time various sportsmen — heavyweights, pipers, dancers, track and field athletes — gathered at the same venue to compete in their own skilled event. It is said that this venue was where the first competitive "Sword Dance" was executed.

St. Margaret's — Scottish Festival and Highland Games, usually held the first Saturday in December in South Carolina, U.S.A.

St. Paul — Scottish Fair, usually held the first Saturday in May in Minnesota, U.S.A.

Step — A change of weight from one foot to the ball of the other foot.

the a.b.c of highland dancing and games directory

Steward — An official, appointed for the purpose of marshalling Highland Dancing competitors at competition and Highland Games.

Stirling — Highland Games, usually held the second Sunday in July.

Stonehaven — Highland Games, usually held the third Sunday in July.

Stone Mountain — Highland Games, usually held the third weekend in October in Georgia, U.S.A.

Stop Timing — is when the dancer stops, holding a position, while the music continues. EG, standing in positions A or D during a "Reel of Tulloch" or "Hullachan."

Straight Lift — The raising of a straight leg to any extended position.

Stranraer — Highland Games, usually held the second Sunday in August.

Strained Muscle — Excessive over-stretching of a muscle causes tearing of the fibre. Stop dancing immediately and rest the affected limb. In severe muscle strains, medical advice may be necessary.

Strathallan — See Bridge of Allan.

Strathardie — Highland Games, usually held the fourth Saturday in August.

Strathconon — Highland Games, usually held the fourth Saturday in July.

Strathdon — See Lonach.

Strathmiglo — Highland Games, usually held the first Saturday in June.

Strathpeffer — Highland Games, usually held the first Saturday in August.

Strathspey — A dance in 4/4 tempo, containing figure-of-eight movements and "Highland Fling" setting steps, performed by 4 dancers.

Strathspey Movement — See Progressive Strathspey Movement.

Style — The general action or bearing a dancer must attain by achieving a distinctive mode of self-expression dissimilar to others.

S.C.D.C. (Stockholm Caledonian Dance Circle) — The S.C.D.C. was established in 1975 in Stockholm, Sweden. Its aims are to practise, teach and perform Scottish Country, Traditional Reels, Hebridean and Highland Dancing, and strive to promote friendship between different Scottish associations within and outside Scandinavia by spreading the Scottish culture.

Stress Fractures — Are the result of continuous impact (hopping, springing etc.), more than the outcome of one definite accident. The dancer will feel an aching and tenderness in the shin and a doctor should be consulted immediately.

the a.b.c of highland dancing and games directory

Summerside — Highland Gathering, usually held the last weekend in June in Prince Edward Island, Canada.

Supporting Foot — The foot supporting the weight of the body is called the supporting foot.

Supreme — Highland Games, usually held the second Saturday in July in Ontario, Canada.

Swing — During bars 1 to 3 the two dancers dance the Propelled Pivot Turn to the right, making approximately 1 and a 1/2 turns (Count 1 and 2 and 3 and 4 and 5 and 6), with a slight extension of the LF after count 6. During bar 4 the dancers relinquish the arm hold and, making approximately 1/4 turn to the right, dance 2 High-Cuts, springing LF, RF (Count 7 and 8 and). During bars 5 to 8 the two dancers dance the Propelled Pivot Turn to the left, making approximately 1 and 3/4 turns (Count 1 and 2 and 3 and 4 and 5 and 6 and 7). Relinquish the arm hold on the count of 7, and continue the movement to finish facing new partners (Count and 8).

Sword Dance — A solo Highland Dance in 4/4 tempo for men, performed over crossed swords, and credited to be the oldest of all the Highland Dances. Like the "Highland Fling" it also has two origins. It was supposed to have been danced before a battle and, if the dancer completed the dance without touching the swords with his feet, the omens were auspicious! Then again, it could even have been the triumphant dance of a warrior who has crossed his sword over that of his fallen enemy! The former explanation is more plausible, as the chief art of today's exponents consist in the dexterity with which the dancer escapes touching one or more of the crossed swords. The steps have undergone considerable variations during its long life — a notable change happening in approximately 1850, before which the steps were danced round the swords by left to right, not anti-clockwise as performed in today's version. See S.O.H.D.A. Dance Sheet No. 5.

Sword Ends — This is the term in the "Sword Dance" used mainly by Highland Dancers in the Southern Hemisphere for where the blade crosses the scabbard out to the sword points. IE, Swords 1, 2, etc.

Swords — A long-bladed weapon used by Highland Dancers over which Solo and Set dances are performed. Either crossed naked blades are used or the scabbard of the sword is placed on the ground and the naked blade placed across it.

Sword Salute — A ritual opening and closing sequence executed before (including the "march on") and after (including the "march off") the performing of the Broadswords. The opening sequence contains the placing of the 4 claymores, while the closing sequence contains the uplifting of the claymores. See S.O.H.D.A. Dance Sheet No. 21.

Sydney — Highland Games, usually held on January 1 (New Year's Day) in New South Wales, Australia.

Syllabus — An instructive list or programme of disciplinary training laid down by an organisation to help further the development of a dancer through various stages of oral and practical examinations.

Syncopated Hop (Movement in "Flora MacDonald's Fancy") On RF — Hop on LF and extend the RF out to 4th Intermediate Aerial Position, then bend the R knee to bring the RF in halfway between 3rd Aerial Position and 4th Intermediate Aerial Position (Count 1). Continue the travel inwards and downwards to place the RF on half-point in 5th Position (Count and). Gently beat the ball of the LF in 5th Rear Position (Count and 2). Repeat as required. See also "Balloné."

T

Tacit — is when the music stops and only the rhythm made by the dancer's feet can be heard. This usually occurs when the accompaniment is played by a Scottish Dance band. The band usually play the first beat of every bar, or every other bar, to help the dancer maintain the rhythm.

Tacking (Arm movement in "Sailors' Hornpipe") — An action during which both hands quickly roll round each other, inwards or outwards. It is used during the Heel-Roll movement, and represents the change of direction of sails or course of the ship.

Tacoma — Highland Games, usually held in mid-June in Washington, U.S.A.

Tail-Coat (garment worn during the "Irish Jig") — A man's formal coat, cutaway at the front and with narrow tails at the back.

Tain — Highland Games, usually held the first Monday in August.

Tam O'Shanter — A cap with a broad circular flat top, worn by the dancer as part of the original costume while performing "The First of August."

Tam O'Shanter — Highland Games, usually held the first Saturday in August in Massachusetts, U.S.A.

Tap — From an aerial position, strike the working foot (toe, ball or heel) sharply on the ground and off again, making a sharp, clear sound — "tap."

Tarland — Highland Games, usually held the second Saturday in August.

Tartan — A woollen (or other) distinctive checked pattern pertaining to an individual Highland clan.

Tauranga — Highland Games, usually held the third weekend in March in Tauranga, North Island, New Zealand.

Taynuilt — Highland Games, usually held the fourth Sunday in July.

Teacher — One who is qualified, through practical and theoretical examination, to instruct, encourage and advise a pupil in the art of Highland Dancing.

Technical Committee — A representation of Teacher and Associate Teacher members selected by a dancing organisation to act as experts in their specialised subject, to discuss, propose and accept adjustments to the existing rules of that body and to make expert decisions on all queries that may arise on the subject of Highland Dancing.

Technique — The skill needed to manipulate the mechanical part of an artistic performance.

Tempo — The speed at which music is played, usually indicated by the stated number of bars to the minute.

Temuka — Caledonian Games, usually held on January 2 in Temuka, South Island, New Zealand.

Texas — Scottish Festival and Highland Games, usually held the first weekend in June in Arlington, Texas, U.S.A.

Theory — An explanation in technical terms of the art of Highland Dancing.

The Thistle — A girl's solo step dance of 6 steps in 3/4 Waltz tempo. The design and formation of each step makes up the various parts of the thistle emblem — the stalk, flower, leaves, etc. See S.O.H.D.A. Dance Sheet No. 17.

Thornton — Highland Games, usually held the first Saturday in July.

Threesome Reel — A dance medley in Strathspey and Reel tempo for three dancers — preferably one gent between two ladies. See S.O.H.D.A. Dance Sheet No. 29.

Tidewater — Highland Games, usually held the fourth Saturday in June in Virginia, U.S.A.

Tights — Although not recommended as part of the Irish National costume, many of today's female dancers wear these pantyhose under their outfit while performing the "Irish Jig."

Time — The sustaining of an equal or methodical space between beats.

Time Signature — An indication of tempos at the start of a line of music.

Tobermory — Highland Games, usually held the third Thursday in July.

Toe — When the tip of the working foot touches the ground in an open position, with an arched instep and a good turn-out, or a closed position with the working foot perpendicular, it is said to be pointed or placed on the toe.

Toe-Heel — Hop on the LF, pointing the R toe in 3rd or 5th Position, Hop on the LF, place the R heel in 3rd or 5th Position; Spring on to the RF, point the L toe in 3rd or 5th Position; Hop on the RF, place the L heel in 3rd or 5th Position (Count 1, 2, 3, 4). This movement may also be danced in 2nd Position and 4th Opposite 5th Position.

Toe-Off (On RF) — Hop on the LF, point the R toe in 5th Position; Hop on the LF, shake the RF out to 4th Aerial Position, 4th Intermediate Aerial Position or 2nd Aerial Position (Count 1, 2).

Tomintoul — Highland Games, usually held the third Saturday in July.

Travel Balance — With the RF extended out to 4th Intermediate Aerial Position, and a slight right shoulder lead, bring the RF in to 5th Position (Count 1); Step the LF back to 4th Rear Intermediate Position (Count and) and close the RF to 5th Position to extend the LF out to 4th Rear Intermediate Aerial Position (Count 2): Bring the LF in to 5th Rear Position (Count 3); Step the RF forward to 4th Intermediate Position (Count and) and close the LF to 5th Rear Position to extend the RF out to 4th Intermediate Aerial Position (Count 4).

Treasure Island — Scottish Games, usually held the second Saturday in November in Florida, U.S.A.

Trenton — Scottish Festival, usually held the third weekend in July in New Jersey, U.S.A.

Triple — A name used by some dancers to describe the shuffle movement, as used in the "Sailors' Hornpipe," "Irish Jig," etc., to differentiate it from the shuffle movement used in the "Seann Triubhas" (Break, etc.) — See Shuffle.

Triple-Beat Rhythm — A musical term where the counting of a movement is broken into 3 beats of equal value. This is not used in Highland Dances but is often executed in the "Irish Jig" and other dances performed in 6/8 tempo and counted as "1 and a." EG, Heel Clips (1st Step "Irish Jig"), Shuffles (2nd Step), etc.

Trophy — An ornament given or received as an award for success in a dancing contest — usually presented to the dancer gaining most points in an individual section.

Trossachs — Highland Games, usually held the second week in July.

Tucson — Highland Games, usually held the third Saturday in October in Arizona, U.S.A.

Tulloch Gorm — A solo Hebridean step dance of 6 steps in 4/4 Strathspey tempo. This dance is sometimes called the "Reel of Tulloch Gorm" and was an earlier form of the "Highland Fling." See S.O.H.D.A. Dance Sheet No. 18.

Turakina — Highland Games, usually held the fourth Saturday in January in Turakina, North Island, New Zealand.

Turn-Out — In attempting to attain the perfectly-executed foot position a good basic turn-out of each foot is essential. The difference between an average dancer and an exceptional dancer can often be detected in their "walk" — the gifted dancer having a natural turn-out of each foot when walking in an ordinary manner.

Turn Over Centre Crossing — This is the term used mainly by Highland Dancers in the Southern Hemisphere for the turning movement executed during Bar 4 of the Open pas de Basque Step in the "Sword Dance." IE, L toe pointed in B in 4th Position (Count 5). Half Turn to right pointing R toe in A in 4th Position (Count 6). L toe pointed in A in 4th Position (Count 7). Quarter turn to the right pointing R toe in B in 2nd Position (Count 8).

Turriff — Highland Games, usually held the first Tuesday in August.

U

Underskirt — A petticoat — a foundation for a dress or skirt — used with National outfit and "Irish Jig" outfit.

U.K.A.P.T.D. (The United Kingdom Alliance of Professional Teachers of Dancing) — Although not a "specialist" Highland Dancing Association, the U.K.A.P.T.D. do have, amongst other branches of dance, a Highland Branch which organises examination and teacher certificate tests in Highland and National Dances.

United Scottish Society's — Highland Games, usually held the last weekend in May in California, U.S.A.

Utah — Highland Games, usually held in mid-June in Utah, U.S.A.

V

Vashon Island — Highland Games, usually held the second Saturday in July in Washington, U.S.A.

Vermont — Highland Games, usually held the third Saturday in June in Vermont, U.S.A.

Victorian Scottish Union (V.S.U.) — Established in 1905, and embracing affiliated Scottish societies throughout the State of Victoria, Australia, the V.S.U. continues to maintain and uphold the traditions of the Scot abroad, encourage the wearing of the national dress and further promote and support the art of Highland Dancing. The V.S.U. and the S.O.H.D.A. are affiliated to each other and continue to exchange information on Highland Dancing through mutual esteem and friendship.

Village Maid — A girl's solo step dance of 6 steps in 2/4 tempo. It was collected in Aberdeenshire by Isobel Cramb, from Thomas Wilson's "Companion to the Ballroom, 1816." See S.O.H.D.A. Dance Sheet No. 13.

Virginia — Scottish Games, usually held the fourth weekend in July in Virginia, U.S.A.

W

Waipu — Highland Games, usually held on January 1 (New Year's Day) in Waipu, North Island, New Zealand.

Waistcoat — Worn by the male dancer as part of the "Irish Jig" outfit — it should be the opposite colour to the tailcoat (red/green), with white or brass buttons.

Walk On and Walk Off — An important ritual concerning the dancer's entrance and exit on and off the dancing platform. When entering and leaving the platform a dancer must walk smartly and briskly with head held high and shoulders back, showing a resolute determination and confident attitude in their step. At many venues throughout the world a dancer's entrance and exit are watched carefully by the adjudicator/s who award or deduct marks for the presentation of their execution.

Warm-Up — It is very important to warm up your muscles through exercise at the beginning of every dance session — this is to get your muscles relaxed and supple.

Waxhaw — Scottish Games, usually held the fourth Saturday in October in North Carolina, U.S.A.

West Texas — Highland Games, usually held the second Saturday in October in Texas, U.S.A.

Whiskey — Highland Games, usually held the first Saturday in April in Pozo, California, U.S.A.

Williamsburg — Scottish Festival, usually held the fourth Saturday in September in Virginia, U.S.A.

Working Foot — While the supporting foot is taking the weight of the body, the other foot is called the working foot.

Workshop — A group of students working on a creative or experimental project.

Wrists — The joint by which the hand is united to the arm. At no time, while executing any arm movement, should either wrist become bent or "broken." The dancer should strive to attain a slight curve of each wrist throughout each performance.

Written Theory — During the full Teachers examination the entrant is requested to complete a written paper on the description of steps.

Y

Yuba Sutter — Highland Games, usually held the first Saturday in October in California, U.S.A.

Z

Zorra — Highland Games, usually held the first Saturday in July in Ontario, Canada.

———oOo———

SCOTTISH HIGHLAND GAMES DIRECTORY

To assist the dancer in selecting the Highland Games at which he or she wishes to compete there follows a list of the relative dates, and contacts, for the Highland Games held throughout the summer months in Scotland.

It is stressed that some months may contain five weekends, so it is advisable for the dancer to contact the appropriate games secretaries to verify dates, starting times, age groups, dances, etc.

We have made every effort to confirm the information and to be as complete as possible. If, however, we have missed out your Games or our information is incorrect, please send details to our publisher and we will endeavour to correct it in any future editions.

Highland Games in Scotland

May

2nd Sunday
Gourock Highland Games
Mr J.A. Douglas
Director of Recreational Services, IDC
Municipal Buildings, Greenock PA15 1LQ
Tel: 0475 - 24400 Ext. 384
Fax: 0475 - 882010.

3rd Sunday
Chirnside Highland Games
Mr Henry Gray
Westerlea, Chirnside, Berwickshire
Tel: 0890 - 818204.

4th Saturday
Bathgate Highland Games
Mr Stephen White
35 Bellsburn Avenue,
Linlithgow EH49 7LD
Tel: 0506 - 670379.

Blackford Highland Games
Mr P. Dobbie
Rattray House
Stirling Street
Blackford PH4 1QA
Tel: 0764 - 682502.

Garnock (Kilbirnie) International Games
Mr D.P. Webster
43 West Road
Irvine KA12 8RE
Tel: 0294 - 72257.

4th Sunday
Blair Atholl International Highland Games
Mr I.G. Armour
Atholl Estates Office
Blair Atholl, Pitlochry,
Perthshire
Tel: 079 - 681355.

June

1st Saturday

Shotts Highland Games
Mr F. Keenan
29 Kilfinnan Road,
Shotts ML7 4JN
Tel: 0501 - 20870.

Strathmiglo Highland Games
Mr D. Mitchell
2 East Mill Court,
Strathmiglo, Fife
Tel: 0337 - 860467.

Bo'ness International Highland Games
Mr Alan Faulds
6 Maidlands, Edinburgh Road
Linlithgow EH49 6AG
Tel: 0506 - 843974
Fax: 031 - 3148237.

Kilmore & Kilbride Highland Games
Mr D. A. Ferguson
Dalantobair
Musdale Road
Kilmore
By Oban PA34 4XX
Tel: 0631 - 77241.

1st Sunday

Blantyre Highland Games
Mr S. Wilkie
Bardykes Farm,
Blantyre
Tel: 0698 - 23564.

Markinch Highland Games
Mr James Duncan
81 Croft Crescent,
Markinch, Fife
Tel: 0592 - 759038.

the a.b.c of highland dancing and games directory

	Carrick Lowland Gathering. Mr Ian Fitsimmons 15 Smith Crescent Girvan, Ayrshire KA26 0DY Tel: 0465 - 2667.
	Eastwood International Highland Games Mr Arthur Segal Parklands Country Club Newton Mearns, Glasgow Tel: 041 - 6399222 Fax: 041 - 6399012.
	Monklands Highland Games Monklands District Council, Coatbridge Tel: 0236 - 762453.
2nd Thursday	**Lanark Highland Games** Mr Millar T. Stoddart Augusta, 30 Gleghorn Road, Lanark Tel: 0555 - 4235.
2nd Week	**Bonnyrigg Rose Highland Games** Mr John Cherrie 26 Polton Street, Bonnyrigg Tel: 031 - 6630464.
2nd Saturday	**Bearsden & Milngavie Highland Games** Mr Walter Boyle The Home Farm Buchanan Castle Estate Drymen G63 0HX Tel: 0360 - 60807.
	Blairmore (Huntly) Highland Games Mrs M. Nagahiro The Old Manse of Bourtie Inverurie Aberdeenshire AB5 0JS Tel: 06512 - 2254.

the a.b.c of highland dancing and games directory

	Paisley International Highland Games Mr D. P. Webster 43 West Road Irvine KA12 8RE Tel: 0294 - 72257.
2nd Sunday	**Ardrossan Highland Games** Miss Ann Clarke Leisure Service Cunninghame District Council Saltcoats Tel: 0294 - 602242.
	Clarkston Highland Games Clarkston Rugby Club Braidholm Road, Giffnock G46 Tel: 031 - 6375850.
	Forfar Highland Games Mr Ken Stephen 41 Clerwood Gardens, Corstophine, Edinburgh EH12 9PX Tel: 031 - 3341365.
	Blantyre International Highland Games Mr D. P. Webster 43 West Road Irvine KA12 8RE Tel: 0294 - 72257.
3rd Saturday	**Campbeltown (& Kintyre) Highland Games** Mr John McLachlan Erinville Dell Road Campbeltown Argyll PA28 6JG Tel: 0586 - 552919
	Lesmahagow Highland Games Helen Small 28 Priory Road, Lesmahagow Tel: 0555 - 892413.

Oldmeldrum Highland Games
Mr Robert A. Forsyth
2 Rosebank, Oldmeldrum
Aberdeenshire AB15 0BE
Tel: 0651 - 873909.

Newburgh Highland Games
Mrs M. Colville
31 Robertson Crescent
Newburgh
Fife KY14 6AW
Tel: 0337 - 840691.

Selkirk Highland Games
Mr A. Douglas
34 Roberts Avenue
Selkirk
Tel: 0750 - 21954.

3rd Sunday

Aberdeen Highland Games
Mr I. McKenzie Smith
City Arts Officer
St Nicholas House
Broad Street
Aberdeen AB9 1XY
Tel: 0224 - 276276 Ext. 2475
Fax: 0224 - 648256.

Falkirk Highland Games
Jane Clark
Kilns House
Kilns Road
Falkirk
Tel: 0324 - 24911.

4th Saturday

Ceres Highland Games
Mr W. T. Brand
Old Manor
Panbride
Carnoustie
Tel: 0241 - 53011.

Cowdenbeath Highland Games
Mrs V. Oliver
5 Lochgelly Road, Cowdenbeath, Fife
Tel: 0383 - 512443,

Drumtochty Highland Games
Mr Alastair Reid
Brodie House,
21 Garvock Street
Laurencekirk AB30 1HD
Tel: 0561 - 377252.

Huntly Highland Games
Miss Betty Jessiman
Morar, 9 Old Road, Huntly
Tel: 0466 - 792409.

Peebles Highland Games
A. A. Fraser
1 Dalatho Crescent
Peebles EH45 8DT
Tel: 0721 - 722024.

Seil Island (Oban) Highland Games
Mr Ron Hetherington
6 Knoc Mhor
Balvicar
Isle of Seil
Tel: 08523 - 246.

4th   Sunday   **Burghead Highland Games**

Grange Highland Games
Mr David J. Dicks
Mill of Paithnick, Grange,
Keith AB5 3LY
Tel: 05425 - 217.

Grantown - on - Spey Highland Games
Molly Duckett
22 South West High Street
Grantown - on - Spey PH26 3QH
Tel: 0479 - 873193.

JULY

1st   Wednesday

Kenmore Highland Games
Mrs Garnett
Kirkton Cottage
Fortingall
Tel: 0887 - 830486.

Mull Children's Highland Games
Mr Wilson
3 St Marys
Tobermory
Isle of Mull PA75 6PY
Tel: 0688 - 2067.

1st   Saturday

Caithness Highland Games
Mrs Pauline Bain
Smithy House
Scotscalder,
Halkirk KW12 6XJ
Tel: 084783 - 643.

Elgin Highland Games
Mrs Janet Valentine
Hawthorne Cottage
Urquhart
By Elgin IV30 3LG
Tel: 0343 - 842578.

Fettercairn Highland Games
Mrs M Thomson
Burn of Balmakelly Cottage
Laurencekirk
Kincardineshire
Tel: 05617 - 583.

Galashiels Highland Games
Mrs J. Walker
184 Wood Street,
Galashiels
Tel: 0896 - 3606.

the a.b.c of highland dancing and games directory

Thornton Highland Games
Mr W. Crawford
43 Donald Crescent
Thornton, Kircaldy
Fife KY7 4AS
Tel: 0592 - 774615.

Kelso Highland Games
Mr John Dawson
28 Dyers Court
Kelso
Tel: 0573 - 224581.

1st Sunday   **Cupar Highland Games**
Mr Alex Mitchell
83 Whitfield Rise
Whitfield, Dundee
Tel: 0382 - 506270.

Dundee Highland Games
Susan Gillan
Dundee District Council,
Earl Grey Place, Dundee
Tel: 0382 - 23141 Ext. 4287.

2nd Tuesday   **Barra Highland Games**
Barra & Vatersay CSS Office
Castlebay
Isle of Barra
Tel: 08714 - 401.

2nd Week   **Trossachs Highland Games**
Mr Douglas Gray
Post House
Brig O' Turk
Callander FK17 8HT
Tel: 08776 - 238.

2nd Saturday   **Alva Highland Games**
Mrs M. Gallagher
7 Aitchison Drive
Larbert FK5 4PB
Tel: 0324 - 558519.

Echt Highland Games
Mrs S. Roger
Tillybrig
Dunecht
Skene
Aberdeenshire AB32 7BA
Tel: 03306 - 276.

Forres Highland Games
Mr M. Scott
7 Fleurs Road,
Forres IV36 0LY
Tel: 0309 - 673289.

Glengarry Highland Games
Mrs C. MacRae
11 Garry Crescent
Invergarry
Inverness - shire PH35 4HG
Tel: 08093 - 322.

Dingwall Highland Games
Mr Alex W. Miller
15 Old Evanton Road
Dingwall IV15 9RA
Tel: 0349 - 62024.

2nd Sunday

Arbroath Highland Games
Mr George Mitchelson
3 Adderley Terrace,
Monifieth DD5 4DQ
Tel: 0382 - 532858.

Stirling Highland Games
Mr M. Kaney
1 Sheriffmuirlands Road
Causewayhead
Stirling
Tel: 0786 - 464880.

the a.b.c of highland dancing and games directory

3rd Monday

Burntisland Highland Games
Mrs Isa Duncanson
31 Kirkbank Road
Burntisland,
Fife KY3 9HZ
Tel: 0592 - 873234.

3rd Tuesday

Inveraray Highland Games
J. R. Wylie
8 Braemar Avenue
Dunblane
FK15 9EB
Tel: 0786 - 823854.

Invergarry Highland Games
See Glengarry

Irvine Highland Games
Mr Ian Strachan
2 Mount View
Dreghorn, Irvine
Ayrshire KA11 4AS
Tel: 0294 - 211905.

3rd Wednesday

Luss Highland Games
Mr J. Fraser Nicol
14 Chapelacre Grove
Helensburgh G84
Tel: 0436 - 72919.

South Uist Highland Games
Mr Martin Matheson
Garrynamonie
South Uist
Tel: 0870 - 60242.

3rd Thursday

Tobermory (Mull) Highland Games
Mr Hugh Kain
9 Rockfield Road,
Tobermory
Isle of Mull PA75 6PN
Tel: 0688 - 2001.

the a.b.c of highland dancing and games directory

3rd   Friday

Dunbeath Highland Games
Mr T. Sutherland
6 Mansfield Terrace
Latheronwheel
Dunbeath
Tel: 05934 - 367.

Kilchoan Highland Games
Fort William & Lochaber Tourist Board
Cameron Centre
Cameron Square
Fort William
Tel: 0397 - 3781.

3rd   Saturday

Balloch Highland Games
Mr John Martin
42 Park Avenue
Balloch,
Dunbartonshire G83 8JS
Tel: 0389 - 52288.

Inverness Highland Games
Mr Robert Steadman
Town House
Inverness IV1 1JJ
Tel. 0463 - 239111 Ext: 262.

Lochcarron Highland Games
Linda Robertson
3 Kirkton Road
Lochcarron IV54 8UF
Tel: 05202 - 539.

New Deer Highland Games
Mrs J. Hepburn
Shevado, Maud
Tel: 0771 - 23556.

Roybridge Friendly Games
Spean Bridge Tourist Information Centre
Spean Bridge
Tel. 0397 - 81576.

North Uist Highland Games
Catherine MacLeod
c/o North Uist Estate Office
Lochmaddy
North Uist, Western isles
Tel: 08763 - 329.

Tomintoul & Strathavon Highland Games
Miss P. E. Grant
18 Main Street
Tomintoul AB37 9BX
Tel: 0807 - 580407.

3rd   Sunday   **Monifieth Lowland Games**
Mr A. W. Johnston
16 Ritchie Avenue
Monifieth
Dundee
Tel: 0382 - 534357.

Rosneath & Clynder Highland Games
Miss K. Grant
44 Argyll Road
Rosneath
Helensburgh
Tel: 0436 - 831555.

Stonehaven Highland Games
Mrs Audrey Lockhead
Kincardine & Deeside District Council,
Viewmount
Arduthie Road
Stonehaven AB3 2DQ
Tel: 0569 - 62001 Ext. 2356
Fax: 0569 - 66549.

4th   Wednesday   **Arisaig Highland Games**
Rev. Thomas Wynne
St Marys
Arisaig PH39 4NN
Tel. 06875 - 223.

4th	Friday	**Durness Highland Games** Mrs J. Cordiner 2 Bard Terrace Durness Lairg IV27 4PN Tel: 0971 - 511358.
4th	Saturday	**Airth Highland Games** Mr A. McGuire 240 Braes View Denny Stirlingshire Tel: 0324 - 824360.

Lewis Highland Games
Events Officer
4 South Beach
Stornoway
Isle of Lewis PA87 2XY
Tel: 0851 - 3088.

Lochearnhead Highland Games
Mrs C. McNally
2 Stathearn View
Millar Street
Crieff PH7 3AJ
Tel: 0764 - 654519.

Southend Highland Games
Mr Archibald McCallum
43 Meadows Avenue
Campbeltown
Argyll
Tel: 0586 - 552750.

Taynuilt Highland Games
Mrs C. A. Thomson
Rathlin
Taynuilt
Argyll PA35 1JW
Tel: 08662 - 431.

Peterhead Highland Games
Mr Fred Duthie
30 Copeman Avenue
Peterhead
Tel: 0779 - 72467.

Banchory Show & Sports
Mr William G. Blackhall
Bogfon
Maryculter
Aberdeen
Tel: 0224 - 733565.

Dufftown Highland Games
Mr A. M. Brown
Ashville
Church Street
Dufftown
Keith   AB55 4AR
Tel: 0340 - 20265/20342.

Lochaber Highland Games
Mr Ian Skinner
4 Pobs Drive, Corpach
Fort William   PH33 7JP
Tel: 0397 - 772885.

Halkirk Highland Games
A. S. Budge
Milton Farm
Halkirk
Caithness
Tel: 084783 - 666.

Harris Highland Games

Strathconon Highland Games
Mr Michael Q. Blackley
East Manse
Strathconon
By Muir of Ord IV6 7QQ
Tel: 09977 - 224.

Callander Highland Games.
Mr Dan McKirken
Dreadnought Hotel
Station Road
Callander
Tel: 0877 - 30184.

Langholm Highland Games
Mr A. Borthwick
Cronksbank Cottage
Langholm DG13 0LL
Tel: 03873 - 80062.

Dunfermline Highland Games
Last Games held in 1989

4th   Sunday

St Andrews Highland Games
Mr Ian B. Grieve
54 Crawford Gardens
St Andrews
Fife KY16 8XQ
Tel: 0334 - 76305.

Glenrothes Highland Games
A. Crawford
146 Forres Drive,
Glenrothes
Fife
Tel: 0592 - 753439.

Rothiemurchus (International) Highland Games
Samantha Faircliff
Rothiemurchus Visitor Centre
By Aviemore PH22 1QH
Tel. 0479 - 810858
Fax: 0479 - 810786.

Aviemore Highland Games
Mr Hamish Davidson
Balmore, Clunas
Nairn IV12 5UT
Tel: 0667 - 52656.

the a.b.c of highland dancing and games directory

Taynuilt Highland Games
Mrs C.A. Thomson
Rathlin
Taynuilt PA35 1JW
Tel: 08662 - 431.

AUGUST
1st Monday

Mallaig & Morar Highland Games
Mallaig Tourist Information Centre
Mallaig
Inverness - shire
Tel: 0687 - 2170.

Tain Highland Games
M. McLeod
Ardvreck
Scotsburn Court
Tain
Tel: 0862 - 893417.

1st Tuesday

Turriff Show & Sports
Mr Eric Mutch
Whitefield, Forglen,
Banff
Banffshire AB45 3XQ
Tel: 0466 - 780267
Fax: 0466 - 780612.

1st Wednesday

Portree (Skye) Highland Games
Mr Allan Stewart
c/o Campbell, Stewart, MacLennan & Co.
8 Wentworth Street
Portree
Isle of Skye IV51 9EJ
Tel: 0478 - 612316.

1st Friday

Dornoch Highland Games
Mr W. Grant
3 Church Street
Dornoch
Sutherland IV25 3LP
Tel: 0862 - 810363.

1st   Saturday

Aberlour & Strathspey Highland Games
Caroline Davey
c/o Aberlour Distillery
Aberlour AB38 9PJ
Tel: 0340 - 871204.

Aboyne Highland Games
Mr Arthur J. Coutts MBE, BEM.
15 Golf Crescent
Aboyne,
Aberdeenshire AB34 5HP
Tel: 03398 - 86187.

Caol (Fort William) Highland Games
Mr Douglas J. Steele
126 Glenkingle Street,
Caol
Nr Fort William
Tel: 0397 - 4421.

Brodick Highland Games
Mr E. Lambie
Tigh - Na - Struthan
Rosaburn
Brodick
Isle of Arran KA27 8DB
Tel: 0770 - 2568.

Dundonald Highland Games
Mr Robert Young
Lynaura
165 Castleview
Dundonald
Ayrshire
Tel: 0563 - 850279.

Glenluce Highland Games
Mrs Cathy Higgins
Newburn
30 Main Street
Glenluce,
Newton Stewart
Tel: 05813 - 235.

Inverkeithing Highland Games
Mr J. MacDonald
17 Struan Place
Inverkeithing
Fife
Tel: 0383 - 414194.

Newtonmore Highland Games
Mrs M. Geddes
Inistrynich
Newtonmore
Inverness - shire PH20 1AR
Tel. 0540 - 673228.

Lorn Show & Sports
Mrs Davis
Anderson & Banks Co.,
4/6 Stevenson Street
Oban
Tel: 0631 - 63158.

Strathpeffer Highland Games
Mr George R. Spark
Glenesk
Strathpeffer
Ross - shire IV14 9AT
Tel: 0997 - 421348.

1st Sunday

Bridge of Allan (Strathallan) Highland Games
Mr John W. Morgan
21 Claremont Drive
Bridge of Allan FK9 4EE
Tel: 041 - 3321234
Fax: 041 - 3325032.

Keith Show & Sports
Mr Ian B. Angus
Seafield Park
Keith
Banffshire AB55 3AJ
Tel: 05422 - 2536.

2nd	Thursday	**Ballater Highland Games** Mr Edward C. Anderson P.O. Box 2 Ballater, Aberdeenshire AB35 5RZ Tel: 03397 - 55771.
2nd	Friday	**Lochinver (Assynt) Highland Games** Wilma Mackay 10 Inverkirkaig Lochinver Sutherland Tel: 05714 - 254.
2nd	Saturday	**Aberfeldy (Atholl and Breadalbane) Highland Games** Mr Moir Bank of Scotland Bank Street, Aberfeldy Tel: 0887 - 820321. **Nairn Highland Games** Miss Eleanor Somerville c/o Nairn Library 68 High Street Nairn IV12 4AU Tel: 0667 - 52367. **Mey (Canisbay) Highland Games** Mr D. Mellor Dunn Watten Caithness KW1 5XN Tel: 0955 - 86220. **Tarland Show & Sports** Mrs P. Reid West Davoch, Tarland Aboyne Tel: 03398 - 81244.

the a.b.c of highland dancing and games directory

2nd Sunday

Aberchirder Show & Sports
Mr R. Paterson
Cranna Bridge
Aberchirder
Tel: 0466 - 780549.

Perth Highland Games
Mr Andrew Rettie
24 Florence Place
Perth PH1 5BH
Tel: 0738 - 627782.

Stranraer (Galloway) Highland Games
Mrs S. Atkinson
Wigtown District Council, District Offices
Church Street
Stranraer DG9 7JQ
Tel: 0776 - 2151.

3rd Friday

Glenisla Highland Games
Mr James Grewar
49 Prosen Road
Kirriemuir DD8 3DR
Tel: 0575 - 73911.

3rd Saturday

Abernethy (Nethybridge) Highland Games
Mr J. Rogerson
Gowanlea
Nethybridge
Inverness - shire PH25 3DR
Tel: 047982 - 411.

Bute (Rothesay) Highland Games
Mr Gordon W. M. Sutherland
Birgidale, Kingarth
Isle of Bute PA20 9PE
Tel: 0700 - 83610.

Crieff Highland Gathering
Mr Andrew Rettie
24 Florence Place
Perth PH1 5BH
Tel: 0738 - 627782.

Glenfinnan Highland Gathering
Mr Ronnie MacKellaig
National Trust Visitor Centre,
Glenfinnan
Tel: 039783 - 250.

Helmsdale Highland Games
Mrs F. Sutherland
Fhearnan
Old Caithness Road
Helmsdale KW8 6JW
Tel: 043 - 12272.

Kinloch Rannoch Highland Games
Mr David Mitchell
3 Bunrannoch Place
Kinloch Rannoch,
By Pitlochry
Perthshire
Tel: 08822 - 343.

Lourin Fair (Old Rayne) Sports
Mrs R. Brothers
Westerton of Logie
Pitcaple
Aberdeenshire
Tel: 04645 - 222.

3rd   Sunday

Cortachy Show & Sports
Mrs Maggi Peters
Cullow Cottage
Dykehead
Kirriemuir
Tel: 05754 - 333.

Montrose Highland Games
Mrs G. Lumgair
South Balmakelly Farm
Marykirk
Laurencekirk AB30 1UR
Tel: 0561 - 377203.

the a.b.c of highland dancing and games directory

4th	Thursday	**Argyllshire (Oban) Highland Gathering** Pauline McKiernan Lyndon Lonan Drive Oban PA34 4NN Tel: 0631 - 62671.
4th	Fri/Saturday	**Dunoon (Cowal) Highland Gathering** Mr Stewart Donald 2 Hanover Street Dunoon Argyll PA23 7AB Tel: 0369 - 3206.
4th	Saturday	**Birnam Highland Games** Mr Ian Donald St Mary's Road Birnam Dunkeld PH8 0BJ Tel: 0350 - 727262.
		Drumnadrochit (Glenurquhart) Highland Games Mr R.T. MacDonald Westfield Lewiston Drumnadrochit Tel: 04562 - 481.
		Invergordon Highland Gathering Mrs Stewart 20 Moss Road Tain Tel: 0862 - 893952.
		Strathardle (Kirkmichael) Highland Gathering Mr Andrew Duncan Ballinloan Kirkmichael Blairgowrie PH10 7LU Tel: 025081 - 370.

the a.b.c of highland dancing and games directory

Lonach (Strathdon) Highland Games
Mr G. C. McIntosh
Don View, Forbestown
Strathdon
Aberdeenshire AB36 8UN
Tel: 09756 - 51302.

4th Sunday **Coatbridge Highland Games**
Mrs Ann Crawford
146 Forres Drive,
Glenrothes, Fife
Tel: 0592 - 753439.

Meadowmill (East Lothian) Highland Games
E. Smith
Leisure & Recreation Dept.,
East Lothian District Council,
Brunton Hall
Musselburgh EH21 6AA
Tel: 031 - 6653711.

SEPTEMBER

1st Saturday **Braemar Royal Highland Gathering**
Mr William A. Meston
Coilacreich
Ballater AB35 5UH
Tel: 03397 - 55377.

1st Sunday **Blairgowrie Highland Games**
P. Carew - Price
Mudhall
Bendochy
By Coupar Angus
Perthsire
Tel: 0828 - 27108.

2nd Saturday **Pitlochry Highland Games**
Mr Douglas W. J. McLauchlan
Easter Auchlatt
Pitlochry
Perthshire PH16 5JL
Tel: 0796 - 472207.

3rd Saturday **Invercharron (Bonar Bridge) Highland Games**
Mrs M. Chalmers
Migdale Mill
Bonar Bridge
Sutherland IV24 3AR
Tel: 08632 - 521.

OVERSEAS HIGHLAND GAMES DIRECTORY

To assist the dancer in selecting the
Highland Games he or she wishes
to attend while on holiday or
touring abroad, there follows a
list of the relative dates, and contacts,
for the Highland Games held throughout
the world during each year.

**It is stressed that some months
may contain five weekends, so it is
advisable for the dancer to contact the
proposed games well in advance to
verify dates, starting times, age groups,
dances etc.**

*We have made every effort to confirm
the information and to be as complete as
possible. If, however, we have missed out
your Games, or our information is incorrect,
please send details to the publisher and
we will endeavour to correct it in any
future editions.*

Highland Games throughout the World

JANUARY

New Year's Day   **South Canterbury Caledonian Games** (N.Z.)
Mr. M. Thin
Langridge
Langridge Road
Temuka
South Island
New Zealand

Sydney Highland Games (N.S.W., Australia)

Waipu Highland Games (N.Z.)
Mrs J Baxter
c/o Picketts
Police Station
Waipu
North Island
New Zealand
Tel: 089 - 432 0210

2nd January   **Temuka Highland Games** (N. Z.)
Mrs R Hix
P. O. Box 116
Temuka
South Island
New Zealand

Last Saturday   **Turakina Highland Games** (N.Z.)
Mr Don J. Fitchet
56A Fox Road
Wanganui
North Island
New Zealand

Last Weekend   **Orlando Highland Games** (U.S.A.)
Mary Fisher
210 N. Lake Court
Kissimmee
Florida 34743
U.S.A.
Tel: 407 - 348 4747

FEBRUARY

3rd Saturday   **Arizona Highland Games** (U.S.A.)
Mr Terry Shelbourne
6724 N. 58th Place
Paradise Valley
Arizona 85253
U.S.A.
Tel: 602 - 948 5453

MARCH

1st Saturday   **South East Florida Scottish Festival** (U.S.A.)
Mr Judson DeCrew
7421 S.W. 146th Avenue
Miami
Florida 33183
U.S.A.
Tel: 305 - 382 2309

2nd Monday   **City of Newtown Highland Games** (Australia)
Mr David Smith
City Manager
P. O. Box 1250
Geelong 3220
Victoria
Australia
Tel: 052 - 22 1033

2nd Saturday   **Ross Highland Games** (Tasmania)

3rd Weekend   **Tauranga Highland Games** (N.Z.)
Mr David Bean
4 Cameron Road
Tauranga
North Island
New Zealand

APRIL

1st Saturday

Honolulu Highland Games (U.S.A.)
Hawaiian Highland Games
P. O. Box 12018
Honolulu 96828 = 1018
U.S.A
Tel: 808 - 524 4468

Natal Scottish Games (South Africa)
Mr Charles Wilson
P. O. Box 31424
Braamfontein 2107
Johannesburg
South Africa
Tel: 9011 - 403 1837

Whiskey Highland Games (California, U.S.A.)
Tel: 805 - 438 5238

2nd Saturday

Dunedin Highland Games (U.S.A.)
A. Keith
1119 Somerset Circle S.
Dunedin
Florida 35528
U.S.A.
Tel: 813 - 733 6240

Eastern Cape Games (South Africa)
Mr Charles Wilson
P. O. Box 31424
Braamfontein 2107
Johannesburg
South Africa
Tel: 9011 - 403 1837

Jacksonville Highland Games (Florida, U.S.A.)

2nd Weekend

Ozark Scottish Festival (U.S.A.)
Ozark Scottish Festival
P. O. Box 2317
Batesville
Arkansas 72503 = 2317
U.S.A.

3rd	Saturday	**Claremore Highland Festival** (Oklahoma, U.S.A.)
3rd	Weekend	**Hastings Highland Games** (N.Z.) Mr K. McMillan 34 Scott Drive Havelock North Hastings North Island New Zealand
		Sacramento Highland Games (California, U.S.A.)
4th	Saturday	**Houston Highland Games** (U.S.A.) Laura Smith 8314 Langdon Houston Texas 77036 U.S.A. Tel: 713 - 772 6956
		South Maryland Highland Games (U.S.A.) Mr Richard Boylan 2602 Apple Way Dunkirk Maryland 20754 U.S.A. Tel: 301 - 855 6101
End	April	**Atlanta Celtic Festival** (Georgia, U.S.A.)

MAY

1st	Saturday	**St Paul Scottish Fair** (U.S.A.) MadisonSheely Macalister College 1600 Grand Avenue St Paul Minnesota 55105 U.S.A. Tel: 612 - 696 6239

the a.b.c of highland dancing and games directory

                        Central Coast Highland Games (U.S.A.)
Martha J. Hagler
1738 Frambuesa Drive
San Luis Obispo
California 93405
U.S.A.
Tel: 805 - 541 6841

Savannah Highland Games (U.S.A.)
Mr John Lamont
2616 Norwood Avenue
Savannah
Georgia 31406
U.S.A.
Tel: 912 - 352 7599

2nd Saturday   **Marin County Highland Games** (U.S.A.)
Mr Jack Sutherland
230 Chapman Drive
Corte Madera
California 94925
U.S.A.
Tel: 415 - 924 0514

2nd Weekend   **Kentucky Scottish Weekend** (U.S.A.)
Jesse W. Andrews
6910 Bridgetown Road
Cincinnati
Ohio 45248
U.S.A.
Tel: 513 - 574 2969

3rd Saturday   **Aurora Highland Games** (Colorado, U.S.A.)

Colonial Highland Games (U.S.A.)
Mr MacLean MacLeod
20 Wakefield Drive
Newark
Delaware 19711
U.S.A.
Tel: 302 - 731 5101

the a.b.c of highland dancing and games directory

Johannesburg Caledonian Games (South Africa)
Mr Charles Wilson
P. O. Box 31424
Bramfontein 2017
Johannesburg
South Africa
Tel: 9011- 403 1837

Rio Grande Valley Highland Games (U.S.A.)
Olive M. Bell
Rt3, Box 3022=B
Albuquerque
New Mexico 87120
U.S.A.
Tel: 505 - 898 1961

3rd Weekend **Great Smoky Mountains Highland Games** (U.S.A.)
Mr Brownlee Reagan
P. O. Box 11
Gatlinburg
Tennessee 37738
U.S.A.
Tel. 615 - 436 5348

Scotchtown Scottish Festival and Games (U.S.A.)
Mr Ron Steele
Scotchtown
Virginia
U.S.A.
Tel: 804 - 883 6917

4th Saturday **Natal South Coast Highland Games** (South Africa)
Mr Charles Wilson
P. O. Box 31424
Braamfontein 2017
Johannesburg
South Africa
Tel: 9011 - 403 1837

Sertoma Highland Games (Ontario, Canada)

| Last Weekend | **Alma Highland Games** (U.S.A.)
Mr Bryan Dinwoody
224 Grant Street
Alma, Michigan 48801
U.S.A.
Tel: 517 - 463 3966

Costa Mesa Highland Games (California, U.S.A.)

United Scottish Society's Highland Games
(California, U.S.A.)

JUNE
1st Saturday

Adirondack Highland Games (U.S.A.)
Mr Harold Kirkpatrick
492 Glen Street
Glen Falls, New York 12807
U.S.A.
Tel: 518 - 793 2903

Bellingham Highland Games (U.S.A.)
Isla Paterson
639 Hunters Pt Drive, Bellingham
Washington 98225
U.S.A.

McHenry Highland Festival (U.S.A.)
Diane Wolfe
Deep Creek Lake = Garret County
Promotion Council
200 S. Third Street
Oakland, Maryland 21550
U.S.A.
Tel: 301 - 334 1948

Milwaukee Highland Games (U.S.A.)
Mr Gary Bottoni
7322 W. Portland
Wauwatosa
Wisconsin 53213
U.S.A.
Tel: 414 - 774 8124

the a.b.c of highland dancing and games directory

1st Saturday   **Modesto Highland Games** (U.S.A.)
                       St. Andrew's Society of Modesto
                       P. O. Box 2545
                       Modesto
                       California 95351
                       U.S.A.

1st Sunday   **Jakarta Highland Games** (Indonesia)
                       A. Macfarlane
                       c/o Lemigas
                       P. O. Box 89/JKT
                       Cipulir Kebayoran Lama
                       Jakarta 1002
                       Indonesia
                       Fax: 62 21 716 150

1st Weekend   **Glasgow Highland Games** (U.S.A.)
                       Glasgow Highland Games Inc.
                       P. O. Box 1373
                       Glasgow
                       Kentucky 42142
                       U.S.A.
                       Tel: 502 - 651 3141

                       Kansas City Highland Games (U.S.A.)
                       P. O. Box 112
                       Shawnee Mission
                       Kansas 66222
                       U.S.A.

                       Texas Scottish Festival and Highland Games
                       (U.S.A.)
                       Mr Ray McDonald
                       3211 Greenbrook Drive
                       Arlington
                       Texas 76016
                       U.S.A.
                       Tel: 817 - 654 2293

the a.b.c of highland dancing and games directory

2nd Saturday	**Billings Highland Games** (Montana, U.S.A.) **Bonnie Brae Highland Games** (U.S.A. Karen Widico Director of Development Bonnie Brae Valley Road Millington New Jersey 07946 U.S.A. **Dutton Highland Games** (Ontario, Canada)
Mid-June	**Tacoma Highland Games** (U.S.A.) Joyce Denton 241 E. 63rd Street Tacoma Washington 98404 U.S.A. **Utah Highland Games** (U.S.A.) Utah Scottish Association 483 8th Avenue Salt Lake City Utah 84103 U.S.A.
3rd Saturday	**Delco Highland Games** (U.S.A.) Mr William M. Reid Jnr. 47 E. Germantown Pike Plymouth Meeting Pennsylvania 19462 U.S.A. Tel: 215 - 825 4381 **Georgetown Highland Games** (Canada) Chamber of Commerce P. O. Box 111 Georgetown Ontario L7G 4TI Canada Tel: 416 - 877 7119

the a.b.c of highland dancing and games directory

Georgina Highland Games (Ontario, Canada)

Illinois St. Andrew's Society Highland Games (U.S.A.)
Mr Wayne Rethford
2800 Des Plaines Avenue
North Riverside
Illinois 60546
U.S.A.
Tel: 708 - 447 5092

Massachusetts Highland Games
(Massachusetts, U.S.A.)

San Diego Highland Games (U.S.A.)
Jean Kelly
1920 Springer Road
San Diego
California 92105
U.S.A.
Tel: 619 - 527 4955

Vermont Highland Games (U.S.A.)
P. O. Box 692
Essex Junction
Vermont 05452
U.S.A.

4th Saturday   **Big Bear Lake Highland Games** (U.S.A.)
Mr Peter W. Crawford
P. O. Box 3255
Big Bear Lake
California 92315
U.S.A.
Tel: 909 - 866 6212

Ohio Highland Games (U.S.A.)
Margaret C. Callander
5135 Kneale Drive
Lyndhurst
Ohio 44124
U.S.A.
Tel: 216 - 449 5373

Tidewater Highland Games (U.S.A.)
Mr William A. Black
5529 Finespun Last
Virginia Beach
Virginia 23455
U.S.A.
Tel: 804 - 396 7182

Last Weekend   **New Brunswick Highland Games** (Canada)
The New Brunswick Tourist Board

Oberlin Highland Games (Ohio, U.S.A.)

Summerside Highland Games (Canada)
The College of Piping
619 Water Street
Summerside
Prince Edward Island C1N 4H8
Canada
Tel: 902 - 436 5377

JULY
1st Saturday   **Antigonish Highland Games** (Canada)
St. Francis Xavier University
P. O. Box 80
Antigonish
Nova Scotia B2G 1CO.
Canada
Tel: 902 - 867 2473

Cobourg Highland Games (Canada)
P. O. Box 424
Cobourg
Ontario K9A 4L1
Canada
Tel: 416 - 372 9813

Collingwood Scottish Festival & Tattoo
(Ontario, Canada)
Kenneth MacIver
Tel: 705 - 445 6704

the a.b.c of highland dancing and games directory

	Manitoba Highland Games (Canada) Mr Don Porter P. O. Box 59 Selkirk Manitoba R1A 2B1 Canada Tel: 482 5726
	Zorra Highland Games (Ontario, Canada)
1st Sunday	**Loch Sloy Highland Games** (Canada) Fort Erie Ontario Canada Tel: 416 - 871 6454
1st Weekend	**Metro Highland Games** (Canada) The North British Society P. O. Box 5125 Station A Halifax Nova Scotia B3L 4M7 Canada
4th July	**Round Hill Highland Games** (U.S.A.) Jean Frame 43 Hoyt Street Darien Connecticut 06820 U.S.A. Tel: 203 - 324 1094
1st Weekend after 4th July	**Grandfather Mountain Highland Games** (U.S.A.) Mr Wallace Stewart P. O. Box 1095 Linville North Carolina 28646 U.S.A. Tel: 704 - 733 1333

the a.b.c of highland dancing and games directory

2nd Saturday	**Athena Caledonian Games** (U.S.A.) Mr Donald R. Duncan P. O. Box 245 Athena, Oregon 97813 U.S.A.
	Haliburton Highland Games (Ontario, Canada) Tel: 1 (800) 461 7677
	Payson Highland Games (U.S.A.) 300 South Payson Utah 84651 U.S.A.
	Supreme Highland Games (Canada) Ruth McNeil 52 Beechwood Cr., Apt. 1 Chatham Ontario N7M 5A8 Canada Tel: 519 - 352 8737
	Vashon Island Highland Games (U.S.A.) Sr. Sterling Hill 10450 15th Avenue S. W. Seattle Washington 98746 U.S.A.
Mid-July	**Shriner's Scottish Games** (Massachusetts, U.S.A.)
3rd Saturday	**Calgary Highland Games** (Alberta, Canada)
	Cambridge Highland Games (Ontario, Canada) R.R#1 Stratford, Ontario N5A 6S2 Canada Tel: 519 - 625 8246

Indiana Highland Games (U.S.A.)
Mr Don Bosse
10419 Cinnamon Tree Place
Fort Wayne
Indiana 46804
U.S.A.
Tel 219 - 436 4363

Pike's Peak Highland Games (U.S.A.)
Wylie D. Reid
542 Lakewood Circle
Colorado Springs
Colorado 80906
U.S.A.
Tel: 719 - 596 3538

Portland Highland Games (Oregon, U.S.A.)
Virginia Johnson
Tel: 503 - 292 2704

3rd	Weekend	**Trenton Scottish Festival** (New Jersey, U.S.A.)
4th	Saturday	**Molson Highland Games** (Ontario, Canada)

Spokane Scottish Festival (U.S.A.)
Mary Alward
418 E. 11th Street
Spokane
Washington 99202
U.S.A.

4th Weekend   **Pacific North - West Highland Games** (U.S.A.)
Sharon McBride-Ritelis
8802 Meridian Avenue N.,
Seattle
Washington 98103
U.S.A.
Tel: 206 - 522 2874

Virginia Scottish Games (U.S.A.)
Mr William P. Sellers IV
2454 Ridgehampton Courts
Reston
Virginia 22901
U.S.A.
Tel: 703 - 860 5227

Final Saturday **Glengarry Highland Games** (Canada)
P. O. Box 341
Maxville
Ontario K0C 1T0
Canada
Tel: 613 - 527 2876

AUGUST
Early August **Alaskan Highland Games** (U.S.A.)
Alaskan Scottish Club
P. O. Box 3471
Anchorage
Alaska 99510
U.S.A.

1st Saturday **Detroit Highland Games** (U.S.A.)
Mr William H. Kincaid
2864 Baylis Court
Ann Arbour
Michigan 48108
U.S.A.
Tel: 313 - 763 1495

Monterey Highland Games (U.S.A.)
Scottish Society of Monterey Peninsula
P. O. Box 1633
Carmel
California 93921
U.S.A.

the a.b.c of highland dancing and games directory

                          Tam O'Shanter Highland Games (U.S.A.)
                          Mr Tom Welsh
                          32 Walnut Street
                          W. Bridgewater
                          Massachusetts 02379
                          U.S.A.
                          Tel: 508 - 584 7116

1st   Weekend   **Montreal Highland Games** (Quebec, Canada)

2nd   Saturday   **Central New York Scottish Games** (U.S.A.)
                          Mr Joseph Walker
                          160 Stafford Avenue
                          Syracuse
                          New York 13206
                          U.S.A.

                          Missoula Scottish Games (Montana, U.S.A.)

2nd   Weekend   **Fergus Highland Games** (Ontario, Canada)
                          Tel: 519 - 843 5020

                          Rocky Mountain Highland Games (U.S.A.)
                          St Andrews Society
                          c/o Charles Todd
                          3606 E. Hindsdale Pk.
                          Littleton, Colorado 80122
                          U.S.A.

3rd   Saturday   **Campbell Highland Games** (U.S.A.)
                          Campbell Chamber of Commerce
                          328 E. Campbell Avenue
                          Campbell
                          California 95008
                          U.S.A.

                          Maine Highland Games (U.S.A.)
                          Mr Arthur Piper
                          RFD 1, Box 312
                          Albion
                          Maine 04910
                          U.S.A.
                          Tel: 207 - 437 2355

| | | **Queechee Scottish Festival** (U.S.A.) |
| | |
Scotland - by - the - Yard
Queechee
Vermont 05059
U.S.A.

Sarnia Highland Games (Ontario, Canada)

4th Saturday   **Long Island Scottish Games** (U.S.A.)
Mr Thomas Richardson
2417 Cottage Place
Greensboro
North Carolina 27455
U.S.A.
Tel: 919 - 282 2832

North Lanark Highland Games (Ontario, Canada)

Last Saturday   **Annapolis Valley Highland Games**
(Nova Scotia, Canada)

Orak Shrine Highland Games (Indiana, U.S.A)

SEPTEMBER
1st Saturday   **Capital District Highland Games** (U.S.A.)
Mr William Munro
40 Terrace Avenue
Albany
New York 12203
U.S.A.
Tel: 518 - 438 4297

Dallas Highland Games (U.S.A.)
Mr Robert C. Forbes
8523 San Leanadro Drive
Dallas
Texas 75218
U.S.A.

Scott's Settlement Festival (Ohio, U.S.A.)

the a.b.c of highland dancing and games directory

1st	Sunday	**Canmore Highland Games** (Alberta, Canada)
1st	Weekend	**Caledonian Club of San Francisco H. G.** (U.S.A.) Mr John Dickson Caledonian Club of San Francisco 13210 Merced Street Richmond, California 94804 U.S.A.
		Santa Rosa Highland Games (California, U.S.A.)
2nd	Saturday	**Ligonier Highland Games** (U.S.A.) Mr David L. Peet 359 Carleton Road Bethal Park Pennsylvania 15102 U.S.A. Tel: 412 - 831 1408
2nd	Weekend	**Blue Ridge Scottish Festival** (U.S.A.) Mr Johnathan A. Collins 2315 Wycliffe Avenue Roanoke Virginia 24014 U.S.A. Tel: 703 - 343 0071
		Long's Peak Scottish Festival (U.S.A.) Mr James A. Durward P. O. Box 1820 Estes Park Colorado 80517 U.S.A. Tel: 303 - 6308 2132
3rd	Saturday	**Alexandria Scottish Fair** (U.S.A.) Virginia Scottish Games Association P. O. Box 1338 Alexandria Virginia 22313 U.S.A.

Amherst Scottish Festival (U.S.A.)
Mr Charles Hutchinson
195 Blake Hill Road
East Aurora
New York 14052
U.S.A.
Tel: 716 - 652 4915

Charleston Highland Games (U.S.A.)
Mr Dewey G. Campbell
P. O. Box 21108
Charleston
South Carolina 29413
U.S.A.
Tel: 803 - 723 2952

Fresno Highland Games (U.S.A.)
Joanna True
P. O. Box 4634
Fresno
California 93744
U.S.A.
Tel: 209 - 226 5708

Loon Mountain Highland Games (U.S.A.)
Evelyn M. E. Murray
37 Blanchard Road
Cambridge
Massachusetts 01238
U.S.A.
Tel. 617 - 864 8945

Oklahoma Highland Games (U.S.A.)
Ruth Rankin
P. O. Box 9796
Tulsa
Oklahoma 74157
U.S.A.
Tel: 918 - 241 6399

3rd Weekend   **New Hampshire Highland Games** (U.S.A.)
                   Mr D. Chaplin III
                   RFD2, Box 608
                   Center Barnstead
                   New Hampshire 03225
                   U.S.A.
                   Tel: 603 - 269 4371

4th Saturday   **Alabama Highland Games** (U.S.A.)
                   Mr William M. Simmons
                   3503 Edgefield Road
                   Montgomery
                   Alabama 36111
                   U.S.A.
                   Tel: 205 - 281 2447

                   Williamsburg Scottish Festival (U.S.A.)
                   Mr Robert Davis III
                   281 E. Queens Drive
                   Williamsburg
                   Virginia 23187
                   U.S.A.
                   Tel: 804 - 229 5653

4th Weekend   **Chevrolet Celtic Classic Highland Games** (U.S.A.)
                   The Celtic Classic
                   437 Main Street
                   Suite 314
                   Bethlehem
                   Pennsylvania 18018
                   U.S.A.

OCTOBER
1st Saturday   **Connecticut Scottish Festival** (U.S.A.)
                   Mairi M. Gray
                   818 Migeon Avenue
                   Torrington
                   Connecticut 06790
                   U.S.A.
                   Tel. 203 - 489 9509

the a.b.c of highland dancing and games directory

Flora MacDonald Highland Games (U.S.A.)
Mr George T. Ammons
P. O. Box 547
Red Springs
North Carolina 28377
U.S.A.
Tel: 919 - 843 5575

Highlands & Islands Assn Highl. Games (U.S.A.)
Missouri
U.S.A.
Tel: 601 - 388 3797

Yuba Sutter Highland Games (California, U.S.A.)

1st   Sunday   **New Jersey Scottish Festival** (U.S.A.)
Mr Peter Mackenzie
33 Beechwood Avenue
Trenton, New Jersey 08618
U.S.A.
Tel: 609 - 882 3010

New South Wales Highland Games (Australia)
New South Wales
Australia
Tel: 02 - 771 3983

1st   Weekend   **Nashville Highland Games** (U.S.A.)
Mr Hugh Gray
20 Academy Place
Nashville,
Tennessee 37210
U.S.A.
Tel: 615 - 254 3500

Pacific Highland Games (U.S.A.)
Cleora A. Lekas-Fraser
21100 Hwy 79, #138
San Jacinto
California 92583
U.S.A.
Tel: 909 - 654 6001

Renaissance Highland Games (U.S.A.)
Novato
California
U.S.A.
Tel: 707 - 539 3326

2nd Saturday   **Anne Arundel Scottish Festival** (U.S.A.)
Mr John Dodds (President)
356 Severn Road
Annapolis, Maryland 21401
U.S.A.
Tel: 301 - 953 1687
Secretary - Ena Koval (263 - 1257)

Lone Star Highland Games (U.S.A.)
Mr Jim Taft
7719 Woodway
Houston
Texas 77063
U.S.A.
Tel: 713 - 785 5092

2nd Saturday   **Norcross Scottish Fair** (U.S.A.)
Georgia
U.S.A.
Tel: 404 - 448 7744

West Texas Highland Games (U.S.A.)
P. O. Box 2081
Lubbock
Texas 79408
U.S.A.

3rd Saturday   **Chicago Scottish Festival** (U.S.A.)
26 E. Atteridge Road
Lake Forest
Illinois 60045
U.S.A.

River Grove Scottish Fair (U.S.A.)
Illinois
U.S.A.
Tel: 708 - 629 2227

Tuscon Highland Games (U.S.A.)
P. O. Box 40665
Tuscon
Arizona 85715
U.S.A.

3rd Weekend   **Loch Prado Highland Games** (U.S.A.)
Mr Floyd K. Ferguson
California
U.S.A.
Tel: 714 - 824 9114

Stone Mountain Highland Games (U.S.A.)
Mr Richard W. Swanson
2010 Innwood Road
Atlanta
Georgia 30329
U.S.A.
Tel: 404 - 636 5308

4th Saturday   **Waxhaw Scottish Games** (U.S.A.)
Mr Scotty Gallamore
3220 Frederick Place
Charlotte
North Carolina 28210
U.S.A.
Tel: 704 - 552 2196

NOVEMBER
1st Saturday   **Jackson Highland Games** (U.S.A.)
Mississippi, U.S.A.
Tel: 601 - 981 5090

Philadelphia/South Jersey Indoor Comp. (U.S.A.)
Marguerite Reid
2913 Benner Street
Philadelphia
Pennsylvania 19149
U.S.A.
Tel: 215 - 535 3907

<u>the a.b.c of highland dancing and games directory</u>

1st	Weekend	**Salado Highland Games** (U.S.A.) Central Texas Area Museum Inc. Salado Texas 76571 U.S.A.
2nd	Saturday	**Pensacola Highland Games** (Florida, U.S.A.) **Treasure Island Scottish Games** (U.S.A.) Mr Jack Wallace 8902 Shady Tree Court Tampa Florida 33634 U.S.A. Tel: 813 - 887 5385
3rd	Weekend	**Shellman Highland Games** (U.S.A.) P. O. Box 532 Shellman Georgia 30324 U.S.A.
4th	Saturday	**Auckland Highland Games** (N.Z.) Mrs Tina Robertson 29 Larnoch Road Henderson Auckland North Island New Zealand

DECEMBER

1st	Saturday	**St Margaret's Scottish Festival Games** (U.S.A.) Mr Bob Hinch 230 Thompson Drive Chesnee South Carolina 29323 U.S.A. Tel: 803 - 461 2888

the a.b.c of highland dancing and games directory

1st Weekend   **Daylesford Highland Games** (Australia)
                            Mrs Wendy Faulkhead
                            P. O. Box 36
                            Daylesford 3460
                            Victoria
                            Australia
                            Tel: 053 - 48 3403

2nd Saturday   **Palmerston North Highland Games** (N.Z.)
                            Mrs Jenny Mair
                            9 Glen Street
                            Palmerston North
                            North Island
                            New Zealand

Hogmanay
(31st December)   **Hamilton Highland Games** (N.Z.)
                            Mr R. Shand
                            P. O. Box 13
                            Fairlie
                            South Island
                            New Zealand

Notes

Notes

OTHER BOOKS PUBLISHED BY
KINMOR MUSIC

THE HARP KEY
24 Scottish harp tunes arranged by Alison Kinnaird

TREE OF STRINGS
Crann nan teud
A history of the harp in Scotland by Keith Sanger & Alison Kinnaird

BATTLEFIELD BAND: Forward with Scotland's Past
90 tunes & 44 songs (both traditional and original) from the repertoire of Scotland's top band.

DOUGIE PINCOCK
The Gem So Small
63 new Pipe tunes composed and collected by Dougie Pincock. With accompanying cassette.

TEMPLE RECORDS
IS OUR ASSOCIATED RECORD COMPANY

Specialising in all the best of Scottish music and song by the following top performers:

- **BATTLEFIELD BAND** • **MAC-TALLA** •
- **ALISON KINNAIRD** • **CHRISTINE PRIMROSE** •
- **ARTHUR CORMACK** • **JIM JOHNSTONE** •
- **EILIDH MACKENZIE** • **Dr. ANGUS MacDONALD** •

For further information on the `real` music of Scotland featuring the best in Scottish harp, pipes, fiddle and voice, please contact:
TEMPLE RECORDS, Shillinghill, Temple, Midlothian, EH23 4SH, Scotland
Tel: 0875 830328 Fax: 0875830392

(And don't forget the Videos by Battlefield Band, Scotland's top band!)